The aim of the B available at the lowest prices new editions of classic titles by well-known scholars. There is a particular emphasis on making these books affordable to Eastern Europe and the Two-Thirds World.

For current listing see overleaf

The Cross of Jesus

Authors in the Biblical Classics Library:

C.K. Barrett
The Signs of an Apostle (19)
F.F. Bruce
Men and Movements in the Primitive Church (13)
The Message of the New Testament (1)
The Pauline Circle (14)
David Burnett
The Healing of the Nations (18)
D.A. Carson
From Triumphalism to Maturity (20)
Jesus and His Friends (15)
The Sermon on the Mount (2)
When Jesus Confronts the World (16)
H.L. Ellison
Men Spake from God (9)
The Message of the Old Testament (3)
John Goldingay
God's Prophet, God's Servant (5)
Graeme Goldsworthy
Gospel and Kingdom (4)
Gospel and Wisdom (10)
The Gospel in Revelation (6)
J.H. Greenlee
Scribes, Scrolls and Scripture (17)
A.M. Hunter
Introducing New Testament Theology (26)
R.T. Kendall
Believing God (11)
Does Jesus Care? (25)
Jonah (12)
Once Saved, Always Saved (28)
I. Howard Marshall
The Work of Christ (7)
Leon Morris
The Cross of Jesus (8)
J.N. Schofield
Introducing Old Testament Theology (27)
Thomas Smail
The Forgotten Father (23)
Helmut Thielicke
A Little Exercise for Young Theologians (24)
John Wenham
Easter Enigma (22)
A.M. Wolters
Creation Regained (21)

The Cross of Jesus

Leon Morris

paternoster
press

Copyright © 1988 Wm. B. Eerdmans Publishing Co.

This edition published 1994
by arrangement with Wm. B. Eerdmans Publishing Co.
Grand Rapids, Michigan, U.S.A.

01 00 99 98 97   7 6 5 4 3 2

British Library Cataloguing in Publication Data

Morris, Leon
    Cross of Jesus. – New ed. – (Biblical Classics Library)
    I. Title II. Series
    248.4

    ISBN 0–85364–628–7

Printed in the U.K. for The Paternoster Press,
P.O. Box 300, Carlisle, Cumbria, CA3 0QS
by Mackays of Chatham PLC, Kent

Contents

Preface

This book arose out of an invitation from the President and Faculty of the Southern Baptist Theological Seminary in Louisville, Kentucky, to deliver the Gheens Lectures for 1988. May I first express my appreciation of the honor the President and Faculty did me in issuing the invitation.

They left the choice of subject to me, of course, but they expressed a preference for something on the death of Christ. It happened that my own thoughts had been running along those lines before I received the invitation. It seems to me that there are aspects of the atonement which have been too little noticed in theological writing and which are very important for the needs of our own day. I recall that Anselm's theory won wide acclamation and that it very well suited an age which was familiar with the penitential disciplines of the church and with the satisfaction for injuries that was so much a part of the feudal system of the day. When later the Reformers took up Anselm's view and remade it into the theory that Christ on the cross paid the penalty for the sins that had broken the law of God, they too were speaking to the needs of their day. At the Reformation period people understood law and the importance of penalty when the law was broken.

Abelard's subjective theory can scarcely be said to be responsive to the thinking of his day, but then it was not widely held in his day. It came into its own in more modern times when the moving power of love came to have a wide appeal. In such a time many were ready to hold that essentially the cross was nothing more than a demonstration of the truth that God has loved us and the result of that demonstration was that sinners are moved to love in return. Perhaps we can say also that Aulen's argument that the "classic" theory of the atonement is that Christ overcame the forces of evil made its appeal to people who in two world wars had come to appreciate the importance of power and the possibilities in victory.

I am not, of course, arguing that these theories were held only because they appealed to something important at certain periods in history. They are very significant theories and deserve to be pondered at every stage of Christian history. I simply notice that what is eternally true may make a particular appeal at a particular time.

And I wonder whether other aspects of the cross will make their appeal to an age like our own. These days people are apt not to be strongly influenced by penitential disciples or feudal satisfactions. Many are not greatly interested in the payment of the price of sin, and a war-weary world may well not be swept off its feet by the thought of victory.

But we experience needs of our own to which the cross gives an answer. To those who ask, "What's the point of it all?" and who are bitterly disillusioned by the frustrations and disappointments of life Paul's teaching that the cross among other things means the overcoming of futility and the giving of meaning to life may come as a breath of fresh air. There are those who are oppressed by the loneliness of it all, when God seems so far away. Human crimes like cruelty and oppression link hands with phenomena of nature like earthquakes and typhoons to leave many asking, "Where is God when there is so much misery?" Does the fact that Jesus cried, "My God, my God, why have you forsaken me?" strike a chord with them? And what of those who are confronted by human selfishness on a large scale, when people exclude from their purview everything but their own comfort and success? Is it meaningful that Jesus lived a life of self-denial, took up a cross of his own, and called on others to carry their crosses? There is much more to the cross than has been made manifest hitherto.

I am not proposing here a new theory of the atonement that may rank in importance with the classical theories. I say no more than that some aspects of the cross have not received the attention they deserve and that some of those aspects may well speak to our age more effectively than to other ages because of the nature of the modern world. In these lectures I have tried to explore a few of these aspects.

In their published form I have expanded the lectures, so that there is more here than was actually spoken in Louisville. In addition I have made some use of material given elsewhere; for example, Chapter One embodies the substance of an article that was first published in the April 17, 1987 edition of *Christianity Today*. And I have added some further thoughts on the general subject. These additions are not unimportant, but this book is basically the Gheens Lectures.

Quotations from the Old Testament are given in the New International Version, but, unless otherwise indicated, I have made my own translation of New Testament passages.

LEON MORRIS

Abbreviations

BAGD   *A Greek-English Lexicon of the New Testament and Other Early Christian Literature* (translation by W. Bauer of *Griechisch-Deutsches Wörterbuch*), ed. by William F. Arndt and F. Wilbur Gingrich; second edn. revised and augmented by F. Wilbur Gingrich and F. W. Danker (Chicago, 1979)

EQ   *The Evangelical Quarterly*

ET   *The Expository Times*

IB   *The Interpreter's Bible*

JBL   *The Journal of Biblical Literature*

NPNF   *The Nicene and Post-Nicene Fathers*

TDNT   *Theological Dictionary of the New Testament* (translation by G. W. Bromiley of *Theologisches Wörterbuch zum Neuen Testament*), 10 vols. (Grand Rapids, 1964-76)

CHAPTER ONE

Why the Cross?

That the cross is crucial to Christianity has never been in doubt for serious students of the New Testament. The Gospels all lead up to it and find their climax there, Acts tells how the first preachers proclaimed what God had done in the cross of Christ, while the Epistles with greater or less emphasis bring out the meaning of this great act of atonement. Through the centuries the greatest minds in the church have turned their attention to what God has done in the cross and have written their profound treatises on it, while on another level the worship of the humblest believers has centred on the cross. Their baptism has been a baptism into Christ's death (Rom. 6:3), and their sacrament of Holy Communion has been a service in which as often as they eat the bread and drink the cup they proclaim the Lord's death till he comes (1 Cor. 11:26). In the study or in the pew the cross has been central. Indeed, so central is it that this fact has made its mark on our language. Whenever we say "The crucial point is this—" or "The crux of the matter is that—", we are saying in effect "Just as the cross is central to Christianity, so is this point central to my argument", for *crux* is the Latin word for "cross" and "crucial" is derived from it. The big question for Christians is "How does the death of Jesus save us?"[1]

1. On the first page of his book on the atonement Martin Hengel says, "In what follows, the most important question that we shall have to answer is: how did it come about that the disciples of Jesus could proclaim that cruel, disastrous execution of their master as the saving event *par excellence?* In

1

The cross is central in the structure of all four Gospels. They have well been described as "Passion narratives with extended introductions". They are not biographies. In each one the death and resurrection of Jesus take up such a disproportionate amount of space that it is quite clear that the author has no intention of giving an account of the life of our Lord. Everything is arranged to lead up to the climax—the cross. They are "Gospels", accounts of the good news of what God has done in Christ to bring about our salvation, and the way the Gospels are put together shows that that means the cross. This is clear also in the rest of the New Testament. The sermons in Acts major on the death and resurrection of Jesus. Paul can sum up the Christian message in the words "We preach Christ crucified" (1 Cor. 1:23). The writer to the Hebrews sees Jesus' coming to earth as "in order that by the grace of God he might taste death for everyone" (Heb. 2:9). In Revelation it is by "the blood of the Lamb" that the mighty multitude are saved (Rev. 7:14). Many more passages could be cited. Everywhere in the New Testament it is emphasized that the cross is at the heart of the faith.

In the modern world this is not always understood as clearly as it might be. Today it is not uncommon to be told that the essence of Christianity is to be found in the Sermon on the Mount, in Jesus' ethical teaching generally, in the idea of liberation, in the thought that God came near to his creation in the incarnation, in "peace on earth", in brotherly love, in newness of life, or the like. I do not wish to denigrate such ideas. Christianity is a profound religion and its teaching has many aspects. But if we are to be true to the New Testament we must see the cross as at the very heart of it all. These other suggestions may have truth in them, but that truth arises from the fact that the cross brings about many changes. New Testament Christianity centers on the cross.

---

other words, how did the crucifixion of Jesus come to take its place at the centre of early Christian preaching? How was it that this infamous death could so quickly be interpreted as a representative, atoning, sacrificial death, and in what interpretative framework was such an understanding possible at all?" (*The Atonement* [London, 1981], p. 1).

Why?

The New Testament writers do not answer this question, at least in set terms. But what they say enables us to discover part at least of the answer. It may be profitable to survey briefly some of the important points these writers make when they write about the cross.

SINNERS

Logically we must start with the fact of sin. This is the basic human problem because it is sin that separates us from God (Isa. 59:2). Dwellers in the space age often view the human predicament as due to lack of education or wealth or resources or the like. The Bible says it is due to sin. The Bible sometimes says that we are all sinners (1 Kings 8:46; Rom. 3:23), and even when such a statement is not made explicitly it is always assumed that sin is universal. This should not be taken as obvious. In the ancient world generally people did not see themselves as sinners; that was a conviction of the biblical writers. And in the modern world it is not uncommon to find people who hold that deep down all people are good. How they do it in the face of the wars, crime, cruelty, selfishness, child abuse, violence, and the policies that allow mass starvation in many lands and the drug culture in others is not easy to understand. Our modern world is almost a classical demonstration of the truth of the Christian contention.

And that sin has more serious consequences than earthly disorder. The Bible speaks often of "the wrath of God" (Rom. 1:18, etc.), and we should not forget that Jesus spoke often of hell (Mark 9:43, 45, 47; Luke 12:5, etc.). Judgment is both a present reality (John 3:19) and a future certainty (Rom. 2:12). We are responsible people and in due course must give account of ourselves to God (Rom. 14:12). We cannot dismiss the evil we do as simply the result of the way we are made, as our fate rather than our fault. That is not what the Bible says, and in our more honest moments it is not what we say either. In the case of any specific sin that we do commit, we know that we need not have done it. It is our fault, and that is our problem when we stand before God.

THE LOVE OF GOD

But the Bible reveals the astounding fact that in the face of our sin God keeps loving us. He keeps loving because he *is* love (1 John 4:8, 16); it is his nature to love. In love he brings about the salvation of sinners (John 3:16; Rom. 5:8). We should be clear about this. Sometimes people set the Father and the Son almost in opposition. They see the Father as a rather stern judge, who sentences sinners to hell. Into this picture comes a loving Son who intervenes to save them. But any view of the atonement that does not see it as coming from the Father's love is wrong.

It is also unbiblical to understand the Father's forgiveness as operating apart from the cross. Modern sentimentalists often think of the Father as a kindly person who does not take sin seriously. "He will forgive; that is what love means" is the thought. But this is to overlook the strong moral demand that runs right through Scripture. The God who demands righteousness from his people is himself righteous, and he does not forgive sin in a way that might be understood to mean that sin does not matter much. God forgives sin by the way of the cross. The New Testament writers constantly hold out the cross as the way of forgiveness; they know no other way.

That, of course, involves the incarnation. Salvation depends on what God has done in Christ. The writer to the Hebrews insists that Jesus was made lower than the angels in order that he might taste death for every one of us (Heb. 2:9), and he goes on to emphasize the importance of Christ's being one with those for whom he died (Heb. 2:11-15). He took on human nature, not that of an angel (v. 16). But, of course, the Godhead of Christ was involved too, as we see from the way Paul intertwines the thoughts of the Godhead and the manhood (Phil. 2:5-11; Col. 1:19-20).

It is easy to overlook one or the other of these. Some modern scholars complain that medieval theories of the atonement put all the stress on the manhood. According to those theories, they say, the man Jesus provided satisfaction for sin and the Father simply accepted it. The Godhead apparently did little. But then they react by putting all the stress on what God has done in winning the victory; they leave little room for the manhood. It is important to preserve the balance. Our salvation is due to none less than God. We must never forget that. And it meant that the Son of God genuinely became man. We must never forget that either. Only by holding both truths can we understand the biblical view of salvation.

THE DEATH OF JESUS

Not much New Testament writing makes sense other than on the basis that God sent his Son to die on a cross and so made a way of forgiveness for sinners. Paul brings this out with special force, but it lies behind what the others have written, too.

This point must be emphasized because there is a tendency in some quarters to stress the incarnation or to take the line that because God is a God of love there is no need for any atoning act. If people repent, he will forgive them. There is both truth and error here. There is truth because anyone who truly repents finds that God is graciously ready to forgive. But God's forgiveness is based on what Christ's death has accomplished, not on any merits of repentance or on some necessity of God's nature. To say that no atoning act is needed is to give us a non-Christian view of salvation. Judaism, for example, could teach that God forgives the genuinely penitent. But to say no more than this is to take up a Jewish, not a Christian position. It is to deny the reality behind all New Testament teaching on the atonement. It is to leave Christ out of the process altogether. Christians must beware of taking up such a calamitous position.

GREAT PICTURE WORDS

To bring out what the death of Christ has done the New Testament writers use some great words, the exact significance of which we may miss since we do not share their thought world. *Redemption* is a case in point. We no longer have the process and therefore it is easy for us to miss what the New Testament writers meant when they used the term. Originally redemption referred to the release of prisoners of war. A ransom price was paid and the prisoners were set free. The word came to be used for the release of slaves (again by payment of a price) and at any rate among the Jews for release from a sentence of death, again by the payment of a price (see Exod. 21:28-30). Sinners are slaves to sin (John 8:34); they are under sentence of death (Rom. 6:23). This way of looking at the cross sees it as the payment of the price that brings us liberty. It tells us that our salvation was at cost and that now we are free, free with the glorious liberty of the children of God.

Propitiation means the turning away of anger, usually by the offering of a gift. The Bible is very clear that God's wrath is exercised towards all evil (Ps. 7:11; Col. 3:6)—sinners face a dismal future. But Christ's death has turned away God's wrath and freed sinners from a dreadful fate (Rom. 3:25; 1 John 2:2; 4:10). These days people don't like the idea of the wrath of God; thus most modern translations have something like "expiation" or "atoning sacrifice" (neither of which involves a dealing with wrath). But this is not the meaning of the Greek words; KJV correctly renders "propitiation", and whether we retain that translation or use another we must safeguard the truth that the wrath of God, that terrible wrath which is exercised towards all evil, is no longer exercised towards those in Christ.

Reconciliation is a homely word for making up after a quarrel. This is brought about by taking away the cause of the quarrel; unless this is done there may be an uneasy truce, but there can be no real reconciliation. In the hostility between God and sinners (Rom. 5:10) the root cause, sin, was put away by the death of Christ and thus the way was clear for reconciliation. Much the same is true of the expression "making peace" (Eph. 2:15); indeed, so closely is Christ involved in the process that he can be said to be "our peace" (Eph. 2:14).

A word that mattered very much to first-century Jews was *covenant*, for they saw themselves and themselves only as the covenant people of God. There are many covenants in the Old Testament, especially important being those God made with Abraham (Gen. 17:1-2, 9-14) and with the people of Israel (Exod. 24:1-8). Unfortunately the people persistently broke this covenant by their sin, and in time God through his prophet Jeremiah promised a new covenant, a covenant that would be inward (for God would write his law on their hearts) and which would have as its basis the divine forgiveness (Jer. 31:31-34). The covenant was at the heart of Israelite religion, for it meant that the people with whom God had made the covenant were his own people; they stood in a relationship to him such as no other people did. When Jesus spoke of his blood as inaugurating the new covenant (Luke 22:20), he was saying in effect that a whole new way of approach to God would be opened up by the death he was about to die. He was saying that not physical Israel but the church was the true covenant people of God.

Justification was a legal concept. We see its meaning in the instruction that in the settlement of legal disputes the judges are to "justify" those in the right and "condemn" the wicked (Deut. 25:1). Paul makes extensive use of this imagery. He sees sinners as facing condemnation when they stand before God. But he also sees God as taking action in the person of his Son whereby all legal claims on those sinners who are in Christ are fully met by his death. There is no further claim. They go free.

Sacrifice was a term that had a universal appeal in the first century. Living as we do in a religious system which finds no place for animal sacrifice, we find it difficult to appreciate the appeal this all-but-universal practice made to the ancients. But right through the known world people stood by their altars in solemn awe before the religious ritual that saw animals slaughtered in their stead and watched as the offering went up in the fires of the altars to the gods they worshipped. For the Christians such sacrifices could never put away sins (Heb. 10:4), but they formed a vivid picture of what Jesus did when he offered himself as a sacrifice (Eph. 5:2). Sometimes they thought of a particular sacrifice such as the Passover (1 Cor. 5:7), or the ceremonies on the Day of Atonement (the letter to the Hebrews uses this symbolism). But mostly they leave it quite general. Everything the sacrifices pointed to but could not effect, that and more Christ did in his death.

There are other ways of looking at the cross. I am not trying to give a complete list, but simply to bring out the point that the first Christians saw the cross as many-sided. In more recent times there has been a tendency to view it from one standpoint only; I cannot but see this as mistaken. The human predicament is complex, and God's saving act that deals with that predicament is correspondingly complex. But, view the human predicament as you will, it was in the cross that the New Testament Christians saw deliverance.

CHRIST, OUR SUBSTITUTE

That Christ in some way stood in our place, was our Substitute when he died, is clear in many places in Scripture. This is strongly denied by some students, and it cannot be said to be a wildly popular view in modern times. But consider the evidence for it. Substitution took place already when Jesus accepted John's baptism, a baptism that numbered him with sinners (Matt. 3:15) and pointed forward to the death he would die for them. Most agree that the Gospels see Jesus as the Suffering Servant of Isaiah 53 who stood in the place of others. Jesus himself said that he would be "a ransom for many" (Mark 10:45), where the word "for" *(anti)* means "in the place of"; it is a substitutionary word. And what else are we to make of the agony in Gethsemane and of the words, "My God, my God, why have you forsaken me?" (Mark 15:34)? Since many lesser people have faced death calmly, it is impossible to hold that Jesus' distress was occasioned by the fear of death. It was not death as such that was the problem, but the kind of death that Jesus would die, a death in which he would be forsaken by the Father, a death in which he took the place of sinners. John records for us the cynical words of Caiaphas, "that one man should die for the people" (John 11:50). He takes these words as a genuine prophecy, in a sense not meant by the high priest, that Jesus would die "not for the the nation only but so that he might gather into one the children of God scattered abroad" (John 11:52). Paul speaks of Jesus as having been made "a curse" for us (Gal. 3:13), and tells us that him who knew no sin God "made sin for us" (2 Cor. 5:21). He says, "one died for all; therefore all died" (2 Cor. 5:14). More could be said, but these passages surely demonstrate that one strand of New Testament teaching insists that Christ took our place when he died for us.

NO OTHER WAY

Was the cross necessary? Was there no other way of salvation? It is shallow thinking to maintain that we can live good enough lives (our whole modern world screams a protest against the view that we are basically good). And it is not much better to interpret the meaning of the cross in terms of its effect on us (in our own strength our response is pathetic). Nor can we take refuge in the idea that the cross defeats evil or gives us power over evil, for that amounts to saying that in the last resort might is right. In the end we are forced to say that evil is a reality and that if it is to be overthrown the right must be vindicated. There are other aspects of New Testament teaching on the cross, and I do not wish to argue that the "rightness" of salvation through the cross is the full explanation. I am simply saying that we cannot dismiss this as unimportant. It is of the first importance.

The deepest thinkers among mankind have always thought that real forgiveness is possible only when due regard is paid to the moral law. C. A. Dinsmore examined such diverse writings as those of Homer, Aeschylus, Sophocles, Dante, Shakespeare, Milton, George Eliot, Hawthorne, Tennyson, and others and came to the conclusion that "It is an axiom in life and in religious thought that there is no reconciliation without satisfaction."[2] Should we not see this as something God has implanted deep down in the human

2. *Atonement in Literature and Life* (Boston and New York, 1906), p. 226.

heart? Faced with a revolting crime even the most careless among us are apt to say, "That deserves to be punished!"

While the New Testament writers do not say this in quite the same way as we do, they do emphasize the moral law and they insist that Christ has brought about salvation in accordance with what is right. Christ stood in our place and endured what we should have endured. There are other ways of looking at salvation, as we have noticed. But we must never overlook the fact that sinners have broken the law of God and that that is serious. If sinners are to be saved, the fact of that broken law must be taken into consideration. It is the witness of the New Testament that Christ saves us in a way that does take that law into consideration. And there is never the slightest indication that anything else than Christ's atoning work can deal with the problem of the evil that is so much part of the human situation.

CHAPTER TWO

Law, Love, and Victory

Despite the centrality of the cross from the earliest days of the church, there has never been agreement on the way the cross saves us. The New Testament has a great deal to say on the subject of salvation through the death of Christ, but it never explains precisely how that death works. When Paul preached in Corinth or in Ephesus, did those who heard him wonder, "How does the death of Jesus in distant Judea so many years ago save me here and now?" If they did, their question is not recorded in the New Testament; nor, of course, is the answer. If anything the question seems to us more difficult still, for we are much more distant, both in time and space, from the physical location of the cross than were the converts of New Testament times. We wonder, we reason, we argue, but there is no answer that is uniformly accepted by Christians.

There seems to have been little discussion of the problem in the early centuries of the church's existence. It was not that the church lacked inquiring minds, for the controversies of those days were many and some of them are the bane of theological students to this day. There were prolonged and profound attempts to answer the questions of Christology—whether Jesus was man or God or both, and how the two could be related in the one person. There were arguments about the nature of the Godhead and whether we should think of a Trinity. And there was much more as the creeds of Christendom slowly took their shape. It would be oversimplifying to claim that there was no discussion of soteriology, the way the cross saves, but it was minimal in comparison to the immense energy that was lavished on other questions in Christian doctrine.

One result of this is that the church has never had an accepted understanding of the way the cross effects atonement. The lengthy and involved controversies in time produced the orthodox statements of Christology and of the Trinity, but there is no equivalent in soteriology. It is true that some views of the atonement are so far from what the New Testament says that the church cannot countenance them, but it is also true that people can profess almost any view of the atonement without branding themselves as heretical.

This does not mean that the church's understanding of what the cross did is chaotic. While there has been no little ingenuity in producing some far-out views on the way salvation works, for the most part theories of the atonement fall into one of three main groups. These are not mutually exclusive, though some have held that the whole truth is contained in one of them. It seems clear to me that there is truth in all three, and I do not wish to abandon any of them. But even when we accept all three, I doubt whether we have come to a final understanding of what the cross did, which may be the reason that soteriological discussion still goes on. But each of these three says something significant, and we may well begin our study by noticing briefly what they tell us.

THE BEARING OF PENALTY

In some form this view has probably always been found in the church. Thus Athanasius remarks that "the Word of God naturally by offering His own temple and corporeal instrument for the life of all satisfied the debt by His death."[1] Similarly Ambrose could say, "as man He bore my grief. . . . Mine was the grief, and mine the heaviness with which He bore it. . . . With me and for me He suffers. . . . In my stead, therefore, and in me He grieved. . . ."[2] This is

1. *De Incarnatione* 9.2; cited from NPNF, IV, p. 41. The editor appends to "life" the footnote: *antipsychon,* a term with vicarious force.

2. *Of the Christian Faith,* II, 53. Cf. also "Jesus Christ came, offered his death for the death of all, and poured out his blood for the blood of all" (*Let-*

not expressed in the exact terms in which the later church expressed the penal theory, but it is essentially the same. Ambrose is referring to Christ as having borne that which he himself deserved to bear. Other statements of this kind may be found in early writers.

But the emergence of the view as a full-fledged theory of the way atonement works is usually traced to Anselm, the great eleventh-century Archbishop of Canterbury. Interestingly he did not try to deduce his theory of the atonement from Scripture. In his Preface he speaks of proving "by necessary reasoning that (Christ being left out of the question as though nothing were known of Him) it is impossible for any man to be saved without Him." In the same spirit he goes on to show that man is constituted in such a way that he should enjoy "a blessed immortality" and that this can be brought about only by a God-man. This approach has sometimes been urged as a reason for rejecting Anselm's whole position, but we should not overlook the fact that this good man was deeply learned in Scripture and that what he found by "necessary reasoning" was not uninfluenced by this fact. Moreover, later writers have found a good deal in Scripture that supports the Anselmian position. In any case we are concerned with whether the theory is true and useful, not how it originated.

Anselm saw sin as an outrage, an insult to the majesty of God. We owe God complete obedience, and when we do not render this obedience we should make satisfaction: "everyone who sins ought to render back to God the honour he has taken away, and this is the *satisfaction* which every sinner ought to make to God."[3] Now an ordinary citizen might perhaps overlook a wrong done to him, but "it is not proper" for God "to remit any irregularity in His kingdom."[4] Anselm's book is in the form of a dialogue with a certain Boso. When Boso says that he thinks he has blotted out one sin by

---

ter 41.7; cited from *The Library of Christian Classics,* V, p. 242). Cf. also Hilary of Poitiers: Christ's suffering "was freely undertaken, and was intended to fulfil a penal function" (on Ps. 53:12).

3. *Cur Deus Homo* i.11.
4. *Ibid.,* i.12.

a single pang of sorrow for it, Anselm asks the searching question, "Have you not yet considered what a heavy weight sin is?"[5] (a question that might well be posed to many who have written on this subject). Anselm proceeds to argue that the only person who ought to make satisfaction for sin is man, and the only one who can do this is God. Thus the answer to the question in the title of his book *Cur Deus Homo?* ("Why did God become Man?") is that Christ became man so that as both God and man he could render the satisfaction that was needed. Christ lived a perfect life and thus it was not necessary for him to die. But he voluntarily gave himself up to death, thereby meriting a great reward which, however, he could not receive, for already he possessed all things. "To whom could he assign the fruit and recompense of His death more suitably than those for whose salvation . . . He made Himself man . . . ?"[6]

Anselm's book is written against a background of medieval ideas about the way kings behave and about the church's understanding of penance, wherein satisfaction was rendered for sins. It is neither to be accepted nor rejected on account of these facts. But we need not be surprised that it seemed more cogent to the people of his day than to some in later times. Thus it has been objected that the great Archbishop saw God as one who had to be reconciled rather than the one who in Christ reconciled the world to himself, and again, that he paid more attention than we would to medieval ideas of merit, so important in the church's penitential discipline. But if we cannot say that he convinces us today so well that we rush to embrace his theory, we can say that Anselm had a better understanding of the seriousness of sin than have many of his detractors. Lochman well refers to "the destructive power of sin and, in consequence, the appalling distress in which the human race finds itself after the plunge into sin, that sin whose depths Anselm plumbed with a profundity unparalleled in the history of theology."[7] Too often in later times people have taken up positions

5. *Ibid.*, i.21.

6. *Ibid.*, ii.19.

7. Jan Milic Lochman, *Reconciliation and Liberation* (Philadelphia, 1980), p. 97.

which reduce sin to the position of a minor hindrance rather than the dreadful disaster it is in Scripture. Anselm also brought out the truths that sinners cannot themselves make satisfaction for sin and that the atonement has a Godward reference.

Indeed, Paul Tillich sees in these facts the reason why Anselm's view "was the most effective one, at least in Western Christianity." He points out that whenever the believing Christian "prays that God may forgive his sins because of the innocent suffering and death of the Christ, he accepts both the demand that he himself suffer infinite punishment and the message that he is released from guilt and punishment by the substitutional suffering of the Christ." He later says, "A system of symbols which gives the individual courage to accept himself in spite of his awareness that he is unacceptable has every chance to be accepted itself."[8] It is the fashion in many quarters today to dismiss Anselm and the Reformers, who took up much of his position.[9] But we should bear in mind that whatever the defects in Anselm's way of putting it, he had a firm grasp on some important Christian truths and some important truths about the way sinful people live and think. We cannot surrender his insights without loss to our understanding of what atonement means.

The Reformers saw the atonement as being effective along some of the same lines as Anselm, but where he thought of God's wounded honor they thought of God's broken law. People sinned and thus incurred the penalty of death (Rom. 6:23). Calvin looks at it this way: "Another branch of our reconciliation was this—that man, who had ruined himself by his own disobedience, should remedy his condition by obedience, should satisfy the justice of

8. Paul Tillich, *Systematic Theology*, II (London, 1957), pp. 199, 200.

9. For example, Gerald O'Collins holds that we can "describe the whole tradition of propitiatory and penal theories of redemption" in these words: "only an angry God can save and only a punishing God can help!" (*The Calvary Christ* [London, 1977], p. 95). Not surprisingly he refers to these views as "such nonsense" (p. 98). But this is no way to treat a view of the atonement that has made and still makes a profound appeal to millions of faithful and thoughtful Christians.

God, and suffer the punishment of his sin. Our Lord then made his appearance as a real man; he put on the character of Adam, and assumed his name, to act as his substitute in his obedience to the Father, to lay down our flesh as the price of satisfaction to the justice of God; and to suffer the punishment which we had deserved, in the same nature in which the offence had been committed."[10] Clearly there are affinities with Anselm, but where the Archbishop was preoccupied with God's honor Calvin was concerned with his justice. He saw the essence of atonement in the bearing of just penalty.

The idea that Christ bore our penalty was widely held among the Reformers, and it is widely held still among evangelicals. It has been subjected to several criticisms, of which we may note the following.

(1) It is pointed out that earthly rulers can choose to be merciful, and questions are asked, "Why does not God simply forgive?" "Cannot he do whatever he wants?" Another way of putting this is to say that the view that Christ bore our penalty makes law, not love, the ruling fact in God's treatment of those he loves. The answer to both the questions, of course, is "Because God is not an arbitrary tyrant. He cannot act out of character." Indeed, Abraham gave the answer to this objection long ago when, in making quite a different point, he asked, "Will not the Judge of all the earth do right?" (Gen. 18:25). It must be said quite firmly that God is not subject to any law outside of his own being, but that does not mean that he is lawless and irresponsible. He is not subject to any law, but law is the way he works.[11] To deny this is simply shallow thinking. Law and love go together, else we do not really have love. Apart from law, how are we to distinguish love from caprice? How do we know that the love we see today will not be replaced by

10. *Institutes of the Christian Religion*, II, xii, 3 (Allen's translation).
11. Cf. R. W. Dale, "The law does not claim Him as the most illustrious and glorious of its subjects; it is supreme in His supremacy. His relationship to the law is not a relation of subjection but of identity" (*The Atonement* [London, 1902], p. 372).

hatred tomorrow? Surely only because there is something of law in the way love works.

We should also beware of confusing love with sentimentality. There is much more of the latter commodity in the modern world than there is of genuine love. Love is concerned for the very best for the loved ones, not for their immediate and temporary satisfaction, and that will sometimes mean taking the hard way of insisting upon discipline and even punishment.

(2) It is urged that, while this theory puts emphasis on justice, in fact it is not *just* that one should suffer in the place of another. But the situation is complicated by the fact that the law in question is the law of God, not man, and that what is obvious enough with our laws may not apply to God's law.[12] The person whose penalty is paid is one who is "in Christ", and Christ is "in" him. We are not referring to some completely external transaction (other than in the sense that the sinner contributes nothing—it is all of Christ), and there seems nothing unjust in penalty being borne for a person who is "in" the One who bears it.

(3) It is further pointed out that Christ's sufferings lasted for a comparatively short time and it is difficult to see them as a substitute for those of people who had merited eternal torment. To this it is retorted that the duration of the suffering is not the relevant thing; the suffering that brings salvation is qualitative rather than quantitative, as the penalty of sin must always be.

(4) It is said that this makes sin something far too external in that it can be transferred from one person to another, whereas as we know it sin is intensely personal. All my yesterdays are mine and no amount of verbal juggling can make them someone else's. But the mutual indwelling of the saved and the Saviour is not to be overlooked or discounted. This theory is not about an external transaction, with sin being taken away from one and given to

12. Karl Barth asks, "Is God unjust?" and answers, "But if we think that He is, what superior justice have we to set against His justice? Is not God the eternal truth of our lives? . . . God does not live by the idea of justice with which we provide Him. He is His own justice" (*The Epistle to the Romans* [London, 1933], p. 76).

another (like a parcel?). It is about the sinner being taken up into
the very being of Christ.

(5) Perhaps the most damaging criticism is that, at least in
some of the ways it has been stated, this theory means setting the
Father and the Son in opposition: the Father demands that sinners
be punished, but the Son intervenes and takes this punishment on
himself. In response to this it can be said that the full deity of the
Son must never be forgotten, nor the oneness of the Father and the
Son. Paul could say, "God was in Christ reconciling the world to
himself" (2 Cor. 5:19). However we understand the cross, it must
be seen as the place where the fully divine Son acted in complete
harmony with the Father to do what was necessary to bring about
salvation.[13]

Such considerations may or may not be regarded as successful
defences of the theory. It is not my intention to try to deal with the
adequacy of such criticisms and defences. I simply point out that
when the debate is over it is still the case that this theory points to
something of permanent value: God saves us in a way that is right.
It is not that God is stronger than the devil and compels him to
release his captives (though there is a measure of truth in this). That
would be open to the objection that it implies that might is right, an
impossible thought for the God of the Bible. Whatever our ultimate
view of the atonement, it must preserve the truth that in saving evil
people God is in the right. He is not simply merciful, for mercy
may be exercised without regard to moral considerations. His
mercy is exercised in a way which preserves the truth that God is

13. Cf. Michael Green, "A clear understanding of this enables us to avoid
the most common objection raised by thoughtful people to an objective
atonement made vicariously for us on the cross by Christ. They say that it
separates the Father from the Son in our redemption. It drives a wedge into
the Godhead. Of course, it does nothing of the sort. Jesus made it abundantly
plain that his death was his Father's will . . . it had been the heartbeat of God
from all eternity. Jesus always did his Father's will. There was no shadow of
divergence in their attitude to Calvary. God was in Christ, reconciling the
world to himself" (*The Empty Cross of Jesus* [London and Downers Grove,
1984], pp. 82f.).

just. He is both "just and the justifier of him that is of faith in Jesus" (Rom. 3:26). Whatever the merits and defects of the penal theory, this is an insight that we must surely preserve at all costs.

A DEMONSTRATION OF LOVE

Abelard, a contemporary of Anselm, set forth a number of ideas about the way of atonement, but the one by which we remember him most is that in which it is a demonstration of the love of God. In his exposition of Romans 3:19-26 he insists that it is the love of God that avails. Thus he says, "'To the showing of his justice'—that is, his love—which, as has been said, justifies us in his sight. In other words, to show forth his love to us, or to convince us how much we ought to love him who 'spared not even his own Son' for us."[14] Later he says, "Now it seems to us that we have been justified by the blood of Christ and reconciled to God in this way: through this unique act of grace manifested to us . . . he has more fully bound us to himself by love; with the result that our hearts should be enkindled by such a gift of divine grace, and true charity should not now shrink from enduring anything for him."[15] Abelard perhaps comes short of saying that the cross does no more than show God's love, but the theory he set forth has at times been expanded in this way. On this view the death of Jesus has no objective effect: it does not pay a penalty or win a victory, other than symbolically. What it does is to show us the greatness of the love of God and move us to love in return. It moves us to love God, and because we love God to love our fellows. When we look at the cross we see ourselves for what we are, sinners, and what our sin has done to God. We are moved to repentance and to love. The atonement avails in the effect it has on us, not in anything accomplished outside us. Sometimes this is put in a form that stresses Christ's example. The cross shows us how we ought to live and

14. *Exposition of the Epistle to the Romans*, on Romans 3:19-26, i (cited from *The Library of Christian Classics*, X, p. 279).

15. *Ibid.*, p. 283.

how we ought to accept suffering, even suffering unjustly afflicted. Or it may be said that when we look at the cross we see what sin did to the spotless Son of God. This moves us to repent and turn away from the sort of thing that put Christ on the cross.

However it is stated, on this view sinners are in no danger, for God loves them and always will. Because of our sin and our finiteness we do not always appreciate this. We tend to be wrapped up in our own concerns. But the cross shows us that the eternal truth that God loves us is far more important than our petty concerns. God suffers in our sufferings, and sometimes this is expressed strongly. I do not think it has been better put than it was by C. A. Dinsmore: "As the flash of the volcano discloses for a few hours the elemental fires at the earth's centre, so the light on Calvary was the bursting forth through historical conditions of the very nature of the Everlasting. There was a cross in the heart of God before there was one planted on the green hill outside of Jerusalem. And now that the cross of wood has been taken down, the one in the heart of God abides, and it will remain so long as there is one sinful soul for whom to suffer."[16] This is finely said and with deep religious feeling. But is that what the New Testament is saying? Does not this way of looking at Calvary effectively take away what P. T. Forsyth called "the cruciality of the cross"? For the New Testament writers what God did on Calvary was of central importance; for Dinsmore and those who think with him it was no more than a moment of revelation of an eternal truth.

It is not difficult to criticize such views. In the first place they are not scriptural. The New Testament does not often connect the love of God with the death of Jesus (though, of course, it does this sometimes, e.g., John 3:16; 1 John 3:16; 4:10), and when it does,

16. C. A. Dinsmore, *Atonement in Literature and Life* (London, 1906), pp. 232f. Similarly H. Bushnell, "there is a cross in God before the wood is seen upon Calvary; hid in God's own virtue itself, struggling on heavily in burdened feeling through all the previous ages, and struggling as heavily now even in the throne of the worlds" (*The Vicarious Sacrifice* [London, 1866], pp. 35f.).

as John Knox puts it, "There is no hint at all that the purpose of the death was to manifest God's love or that its effectiveness for our salvation lies in any degree in this disclosure."[17] In any case it has not been shown that the revelation of love can take place in something that is simply a gesture. The illustration has been used of a man who jumps into a rushing stream to show his love for me. If I am in the water in danger of drowning, that is meaningful. But if I am quite safe, sitting on the pier and enjoying the sun, then I cannot but deplore his action and I fail to see how it in fact shows his love. If sinners were in no danger on account of their sin, then why should Jesus have died at all? In that case we need an act of revelation, but not an act of atonement. It seems that no understanding of the cross is going to be satisfactory that does not view the death of Christ as accomplishing something. The New Testament speaks of redemption, reconciliation, propitiation, the making of a new covenant, justification, and more. In the face of such evidence it is not possible to reduce the atonement to a demonstration of something that was always true. This view, moreover, does not speak of an overcoming of evil, but simply of bypassing it. Any overcoming is done by the sinner turning away from it. This is not the way the New Testament looks at it. Moreover, this view has "nothing to say to the already penitent sinner who is concerned about the evil forces he has set in motion", as Hodgson puts it.[18] Such a sinner knows that he is guilty of wronging others, but on this view nobody does anything about this. The sinner knows that God loves him, but his wrongdoing remains. Some variant of the view has been very popular in modern times, but that reflects our concern for love and our distaste for propitiation, the payment of penalty, the bearing of sin, and the like. As a serious contender for a genuinely Christian understanding of the death of Jesus this view must be dismissed.

And yet. And yet. It is certainly true that "God commends his

17. John Knox, *The Death of Christ* (London, 1959), p. 147.

18. Leonard Hodgson, *The Doctrine of the Atonement* (London, 1951), p. 82.

own love toward us in that while we were still sinners Christ died for us" (Rom. 5:8). And it is also true that "Greater love no one has than this, that one lay down his life for his friends" (John 15:13). John assures us that "In this we know love, that he laid down his life for us" (1 John 3:16), and again, "Herein is love, not that *we* loved God but that *he* loved us and sent his Son to be the propitiation for our sins" (1 John 4:10). That the love of God is tied up intimately with the cross of Christ is one of the precious teachings of the New Testament and one that has left its mark on Christian piety. Take such a hymn as "When I Survey the Wondrous Cross"; go through it line by line and verse by verse and you will find nothing but the subjective view of the cross. The hymn writer says nothing about anything the cross does outside the sinner. Yet we all sing this with wholehearted acceptance. It rings true. While we cannot accept the view as a satisfying understanding of the atonement in itself, yet it contains a truth we cannot do without. At the end of the day the great and wonderful truth is that God loves even sinful people.

VICTORY

In our century Gustav Aulen has written compellingly about what he calls the "classic" theory, the view that the essential thing in the atonement is Christ's victory over evil. He finds the note of victory in the writers of the early church and, though somewhat muted, in the Reformation period, and even in modern times. It has always found its way into our Easter hymns, in which we celebrate the resurrection, Christ's victory over death.

We may approach the subject this way. In the early church people were very conscious of the reality of Satan and firmly believed that sinners are condemned to come under Satan's torments in hell. Now there is a strand of scriptural teaching that speaks of Jesus as having contact after his death with the spirits in prison (1 Pet. 3:19; 4:6) and the creeds of the church could say, "he descended into hell". There is another strand that speaks of Christ as effecting redemption (Eph. 1:7) and of being himself a "ransom" for his people (Mark 10:45). All this could be put together in some such way as this: Because we sinned we passed into Satan's possession. But God, so to speak, made a bargain with Satan. He agreed to give his Son as a ransom for the sinners in Satan's possession. Satan, of course, eagerly accepted the bargain, for in Christ he was getting greater value than that of all the sinners he held. So what happened on Calvary was that Christ was handed over to Satan. But then the evil one found that he could not hold his new captive. On that first Easter Day Christ burst the bonds of hell and rose triumphant. Satan was left lamenting, minus both his first captives and him whom he had accepted as a ransom.

It did not require profound thinking to see that the omniscient God must have known that this would happen. In offering his bargain it seems that he deceived Satan. But, bless you, that did not faze the early church fathers in the least. They gloried in it. It simply showed that God was wiser than Satan as well as stronger. Gregory of Nyssa could liken what happened to a fishing trip: "in order to secure that the ransom in our behalf might be easily accepted by him who required it, the Deity was hidden under the veil of our nature, that so, as with ravenous fish, the hook of the Deity might be gulped down along with the bait of flesh, and thus, life being introduced into the house of death, and light shining in darkness, that which is diametrically opposed to light and life might vanish; for it is not in the nature of darkness to remain when light is present, or of death to exist when life is active."[19] The great Augustine simply exchanged the fishhook for the mousetrap, but had essentially the same idea.[20] It was the grotesqueness of such imagery that in due time caused the church to abandon this way of looking at the atonement. Nobody who read Anselm with understanding could take seriously the idea that God played games with Satan and outwitted him. What Aulen has done has been to show that, while the fathers used grotesque and unacceptable imagery,

19. *The Great Catechism* xxiv.

20. In Sermon lxxx.2 on John 6:9 he says, "And what did our Redeemer to him who held us captive? For our ransom he held out His Cross as a trap; he placed in It as a bait His Blood."

underlying it all is a valid idea, the idea that in the death and resurrection God in Christ defeated all the forces of evil. This is to be seen in some parts of the New Testament, for example, when Paul writes that Christ, having "stripped off the powers and the authorities, made a spectacle of them, having triumphed over them" (Col. 2:15). The defeat of the powers of evil is a genuine part of New Testament teaching.[21]

Like the other views we have looked at, this one may legitimately be criticized. It has been objected that Aulen has simply replaced the legal imagery of the Reformers with military imagery, picturing a battle rather than a lawsuit. And if the battle has been fought and the victory won, the question immediately arises, Why is evil so strong? Evil seems more powerful and more widespread than it ever was. The continuing vitality of evil is, of course, a problem on any theory of the atonement, but it is a special problem for a theory that puts all its emphasis on victory. Again, while there is no great problem in seeing Jesus' resurrection as a defeat of death, it is not easy to see how it can mean a victory over Satan. Or if we prefer to think of the forces of evil impersonally rather than of a personal devil, it is not at all obvious how the resurrection of the Son of God means a victory over evil.[22] A further objection is that this theory says nothing about the past. Do the sins already committed not matter? Should they not be atoned for in some way? It may well be held that this view draws attention to an important aspect of what salvation means, but it is not easy to

21. Cf. Ethelbert Stauffer: Christ's "redemptive work embraces both heaven and earth (Col. 1.20). The crucified has disarmed the principalities and powers, and led them in his triumphal procession (Col. 2.15). Therefore, Christ is Lord not only of his Church, but of the whole cosmos, and all its powers (Col. 2.10)" (New Testament Theology [London, 1955], p. 39).

22. Cf. Alan Richardson, "it would be better to say that the idea of Christus Victor is concerned with the creation-salvation concept rather than with that of atonement for sin; or we might say that it is concerned with the defeat and destruction of the alien (non-human) 'powers' rather than with the reconciliation of rebellious and sinful men to the holy God" (An Introduction to the Theology of the New Testament [London, 1958], p. 205).

find in it a real explanation of the way atonement is brought about. That the atonement includes an element of victory we may well agree. That Aulen's theory is an acceptable account of the whole process we must reject.

There is a fairly general feeling in modern times that no one theory takes account of all the facts. We need elements from more than one of them to account for the varied teaching of the New Testament. Thus we cannot regard a theory as acceptable if it does not safeguard the thought that God acts rightly in the manner in which he saves us, if it does not underline the truth that it is only because God loves us that we are saved, if it does not bring before us the mighty triumph that Christ has wrought on our behalf. While it is my personal conviction that some form of the penal theory is the most acceptable single view, I am also of the opinion that elements of the other views are important and must not be lost.

Perhaps we should cast our nets a little wider than did those who evolved the traditional theories. Dr Frances Young remarks that "What the early Fathers of the church were deeply aware of was the fact that man's problem is not just sin—it is not just a moral problem as the Western approaches to atonement tend to assume." At this point I am tempted to ask, with Anselm, "Have you not yet considered what a heavy weight sin is?" We must not take up an attitude to sin that makes it seem comparatively unimportant. It is a very heavy weight, and theories of the atonement have done right when they have given a good deal of attention to it. But Dr Young's further point is well worth serious attention. She says, "There is something in the present constitution of creation as a whole which is corrupt. Sin is one symptom of a deeper problem— the problem of ignorance, weakness and sheer powerlessness, the problem of perversity, the problem of sickness, decay and death— the profound resistance of man and his environment to full and enduring life and peace."[23] In Scripture some of these problems are connected with Christ's saving work, and it may well be that we

23. Frances Young, *Can These Bones Live?* (London, 1982), p. 36.

should take them into consideration when we are considering what the atonement means.

It is also worth remembering that the various theories seem to have been evolved against the background of the ideas that were widely accepted at the time they appeared or in the period when they won wide acceptance. The early church delighted in the thought of ransom and found imagery drawn from that process more congenial than we do. The medieval church placed a lot of emphasis on satisfaction, which fitted in with contemporary penitential practice and with feudal ideas of honour. The age of liberalism found it congenial to think of atonement as a subjective process in which we can dwell on the miracle of God's love for sinners.

Is there any possibility that the modern church could find some aspects of New Testament teaching that link the atonement with ideas congenial to us? It seems to me that there are some teachings to which insufficient attention has been given, but which speak to concerns of those who live in our age. Perhaps just as the standard theories need to be supplemented by one another, so in modern times there are aspects of the atonement that are a little more obvious than they have been in an earlier age and which we may usefully add to what we know of atonement.

CHAPTER THREE

The Answer to Futility

"The creation", Paul writes, "was subjected to futility [or, 'to frustration', BAGD], not of its own will but on account of him who subjected it in hope. For the creation itself will be freed from slavery to corruption into the liberty of the glory of the children of God. For we know that all the creation groans together and travails together until now" (Rom. 8:20-22). Some scholars see a reference to mankind, possibly especially to unregenerate mankind, in these words.[1] But it is hard to believe that this was Paul's meaning. He cannot be referring to the regenerate, for he differentiates the saved from "the whole creation" (vv. 22-23). Nor can he mean the unregenerate, for he does not regard them as being brought into the liberty of the glory of the sons of God (v. 21). It is unlikely that the words refer to good angels, for they were not subjected to the futility of which Paul writes, or to evil angels, for they are not looking forward to the revelation of the sons of God. Paul is surely referring to the whole of creation below the personal level; he is speaking of animals and birds and trees and flowers, of rocks and

1. E. Käsemann notices scholars who conduct a "passionate plea" for "the world of mankind" as the meaning, and he himself does not doubt "that non-Christians are included" (*Commentary on Romans* [Grand Rapids, 1980], pp. 232f.; he goes on to note that there is an emphasis on "non-human creation"). John G. Gager cites approvingly H. Hommel for the view that in Paul the "primary reference has become the nonbelieving, human world" (JBL, LXXXIX [1970], p. 329).

soil and rivers and seas. And if this is not the kind of thing we would say, we must bear in mind that Scripture speaks of trees singing for joy (Ps. 96:12) and clapping their hands (Isa. 55:12; rivers clap their hands as well [Ps. 98:8]), of the wilderness rejoicing (Isa. 35:1), of the mountains and hills bursting into song (Isa. 55:12), and much more. Neither Paul nor any of these Old Testament writers, of course, is speaking of a conscious process. They are using personification, but drawing attention to the fact that all of nature has its place in God's purpose.

The creation narrative tells us that when everything had been brought into being, God "saw all that he had made, and it was very good" (Gen. 1:31). The human race was given mastery over this perfect creation (Gen. 1:28), but in due course our first parents sinned and this had calamitous effects on nature as well as on them. After Adam and Eve had sinned, God said to Adam, "Cursed is the ground because of you . . ." (Gen. 3:17). Paul clearly has this in mind when he speaks of nature as being in slavery to corruption and as groaning and travailing right up to the time he wrote (Rom. 8:21-22). Richard Bauckham gives an excellent summary of the situation when he says: "since humanity is the dominant species on earth human sin is bound to have very widespread effects on nature as a whole. The fall disturbed humanity's harmonious relationship with nature, alienating us from nature, so that we now experience nature as hostile, and introducing elements of struggle and violence into our relationship with nature (Gen. 3:15, 17-19; 9:2). Because we misuse nature, nature suffers and awaits our full redemption. . . ."[2]

A frightening amount of the trouble in nature can be attributed to the activities of the human race. There is a strong temptation to exploit nature, and we have done this from very early times. We cut down forests and create dust bowls. We remove the soil cover and create soil erosion. We adopt harsh policies towards some species and wipe them out. With incredible recklessness we squander earth's nonrenewable resources. A nuclear holocaust, which could

2. EQ, LVIII (1986), p. 240.

result from one of our more striking modern achievements, is a threat to all life on earth. There is no question but that our attitude towards friend Earth has had frightfully damaging consequences. The frustration of which Paul writes comes about in our day because (a) unless we use nature we cannot live at all, and (b) if we do not use nature properly we ruin it, but (c) we do not know where the balance lies.

Not all the problems we observe in nature are, of course, the result of our sin. There is a good deal of cruelty in "Nature, red in tooth and claw", as anyone who has seen a cat playing with a mouse will immediately realize. And there is the awe-inspiring destructive power of a volcano or a typhoon or an earthquake. But our lives can be affected by many such aspects of the world in which we live, and it is part of our frustration that there is little we can do about them. A "Be kind to animals week" may affect our behavior, but it will do nothing to persuade animals to be kind to one another. And no matter how pure our attitude towards nature, it will not affect our fate when the earthquake strikes. Living on this earth can be a frustrating business.

Frustration arises because we are part of this physical creation. Our minds constantly inform us of desirable things to do which our bodies simply will not let us perform. Some of us would like to be world class athletes, but, train as we will, we never attain the performance we long for. Some of us would like to be great painters but our hands will not cooperate, great singers but our throats let us down. Day by day we find that we are not strong enough or not tall enough or not short enough or not heavy enough or too heavy. And if we move from things that will forever be impossible for us, we all find that at times we are confronted with things that we know are within our physical capacity, but at the moment we are too tired to do them, or perhaps sickness or something else inhibits us. Bodily life is a frustrating business, and we all know this only too well.

CHANGE AND DECAY

In Romans 8 Paul points to another truth we all recognize, that decay runs through the whole of life. Our bodies are such that in a sense they are decaying all the time and in the end our ability to replace what has decayed is diminished and we die. We must face the fact that unless the parousia takes place soon our whole physical organism and that of all our friends is destined to decay. This is not something peculiar to human life but something we share with all creation. Indeed, in this passage Paul is referring more particularly to nonhuman creation. Our scientists tell us that the entire universe is subject to change; it is steadily running down. Paul says that the entire creation "groans together and travails together until now" (v. 22). He is referring to the physical universe but also specifically to human bodies, for he says, "we ourselves [there is emphasis on the subject] groan within ourselves" (v. 23). We may not like it, but it is a fact of life (and, of course, of death).

Some expositors "spiritualize" the passage and take "futility" as a use of the abstract for the concrete; they regard it as a reference to people of a particular cast of mind, perhaps the idolaters of Romans 1:21 (where the cognate verb is used). This is most unlikely. A better suggestion is that the reference is to Ecclesiastes, where the word is used of the futility of all human affairs.[3] But while Paul would doubtless have been very ready to refer to that futility, he does seem to be referring here to subhuman creation rather than to human affairs. C. E. B. Cranfield understands it in this way, and goes on: "We may think of the whole magnificent theatre of the universe together with all its splendid properties and all the chorus

3. The correct translation of *hebel* in Ecclesiastes is a matter of considerable debate, but certainly "futility" fits many contexts. Michael V. Fox argues for "absurd" as the basic idea (JBL, 105 [1986], pp. 409-27). He can say, "Qohelet speaks of futile activities not to warn against those activities so much as to muster the fact of that futility as evidence for his contention that life is absurd"; he goes on to speak of "the irrationality of life as a whole" (p. 426). F. Brown, S. R. Driver, and C. A. Briggs understand the word as used in Ecclesiastes to mean "the fruitlessness of all human enterprise and endeavour" (*A Hebrew and English Lexicon of the Old Testament* [Oxford, 1907], p. 210).

of sub-human life, created to glorify God but unable to do so fully, so long as man the chief actor in the drama of God's praise fails to contribute his rational part."[4] We must not let ourselves be deceived by our physical insignificance against the backdrop of an immense universe. Was it Pascal who said that if the whole universe united to crush a man the man would still be nobler than the universe because he would know that he was crushed? The human race has clearly been given a very important part to play in whatever the universe is for, and I do not see how it can seriously be disputed that as long as the human race fails to glorify God the universe lacks its perfection. We should take seriously Paul's point that there is that which is incomplete throughout the whole universe. Until it is redeemed frustration and decay are bound up with all existence.

Paul goes on to speak of "the redemption of our body" (v. 23), that part of us which has such immediate and obvious connection with the rest of nature. "Redemption", as Paul uses it, is a word that points to the price Christ paid on the cross to bring us deliverance, so this passage must be included among those that refer to the atonement. His words about a "natural" body and a "spiritual" body in 1 Corinthians 15 make it clear that this is not to be interpreted in a crude, materialistic sense. But it is not to be watered down either. He is saying that bodily values will be preserved at the resurrection. Just as our sin has affected all nature, so our redemp-

4. C. E. B. Cranfield, *A Critical and Exegetical Commentary on the Epistle to the Romans*, I (Edinburgh, 1975), p. 414. Elsewhere Cranfield also says, "And, if the question is asked, 'What sense can there be in saying that the sub-human creation—the Jungfrau, for example, or the Matterhorn, or the planet Venus—suffers frustration by being prevented from properly fulfilling the purpose of its existence?', the answer must surely be that the whole magnificent theatre of the universe, together with all its splendid properties and all the varied chorus of sub-human life, created for God's glory, is cheated of its true fulfilment so long as man, the chief actor in the great drama of God's praise, fails to contribute his rational part" (*Reconciliation and Hope,* ed. Robert Banks [Grand Rapids and Exeter, 1974], p. 227)

tion will have its effects on nature, too.[5] Salvation has as one of its
effects the restoration of the damage caused by sin, and that in nature as well as in the human race.

But it may well be that it does more than this. Paul speaks of
creation as being subjected to futility, but "in hope" (v. 20).[6] Now
for the apostle hope is closely bound up with the work of Christ; it
is "the hope of the gospel" (Col. 1:23), it is "Christ in you, the hope
of glory" (Col. 1:27), the helmet of the Christian is "the hope of
salvation" (1 Thess. 5:8), for those justified by the grace of Jesus
Christ our Saviour there is the "hope of eternal life" (Tit. 3:7). A little later in this passage Paul points out that we are saved in hope
and insists that this points to something future—we do not hope for
what we already have and now we hope steadfastly for something
yet to come (vv. 24-25). The implication appears to be that Paul
sees salvation as doing more than restore creation to what it was
before it experienced sin's calamitous effects.

This is supported by the fact that "the whole creation groans
together and travails together" (v. 22). Paul uses compound verbs
to underline his point that the whole of creation is caught up in the
groaning and travailing of which he writes. This is not some mere
local and partial affair. "Travails" is the word employed for the

5. "Even now man, who by selfish exploitation can turn the good earth
into a dust bowl, can by responsible stewardship make the desert blossom like
the rose; what then will be the effect of a completely redeemed humanity on
the creation entrusted to its care?" (F. F. Bruce, *The Letter of Paul to the
Romans*[2] [London, 1985], pp. 160f.).

6. The notion of hope is sometimes found in Jewish writings; for example, "there is the new world which does not carry back to corruption those
who enter into its beginning" (2 Baruch 44:12; the same book has its vision
of a time when "on one vine will be a thousand branches, and one branch will
produce a thousand clusters, and one cluster will produce a thousand grapes,
and one grape will produce a cor of wine" [29:5]). See also Sibylline Oracles
3:620, 744-56. Such writings do not, of course, provide parallels to what Paul
is saying, but they do indicate that the hope of great blessing in God's
kingdom to be set up at some time in the future was to be found among the
Jews.

pains of childbirth, a metaphor used a number of times in the Old Testament for "public distress, anxiety and affliction in times of war or national struggles, or anxiety and fear at God's wrath and judgment"; it is "so often used for annihilating disasters and divine judgments".[7] Jesus used the metaphor for the ushering in of the final state of blessing (Mark 13:8).[8] So here the thought is that the anguish of which Paul writes is not meaningless: it will issue in due course in final blessing. It indicates the judgment of God upon a sinful world, but it indicates also that judgment is not God's last word. Blessing will emerge out of the present suffering.

It is a vivid and picturesque metaphor, but we must not press it too far. Paul is not saying that creation will produce a new order in itself, out of its own birth pangs. Creation itself is not responsible for the new creation. Paul is saying that the birth pangs are a sign of the judgment of God, a judgment that has its effect on the whole of creation. They are a sign also of hope, but of hope that comes, not from the judgment and the suffering that creation itself endures, but from Christ's identification of himself with all our need, seen in the judgment and the suffering. It is his sufferings that bring about the redemption (including the redemption of the body [v. 23]), his sufferings not ours.

Creation has been disturbed and thrown out of kilter by the coming of sin. Paul emphasizes that this has its effects on all that exists. It is part of the human condition that we must live out our lives in a fallen creation. But the very language in which Paul brings out the futility and frustration that mark creation points also to the truth that this is not the whole story. The saving work of

7. G. Bertram, *TDNT*, IX, pp. 669, 670.

8. Cranfield cites A. Schlatter, "To understand aright the significance of the metaphor, one must remember what motherhood meant for the Jewish woman. Without it her life was robbed of its goal and substance. The beginning of travail marked the end of the disgrace that rested on the childless woman, the approaching fulfilment of her strongest desire. It begins with grievous pains, but these pains are to her the promise of that for which she has waited with longing" (C. E. B. Cranfield, *The Gospel according to Saint Mark* [Cambridge, 1959], p. 396).

Christ, looked at from one point of view, is a dealing with that futility and frustration. The suffering he bore is in one sense part of the universal suffering and groaning and in another sense the result of God's judgment on evil.[9] And it is a suffering that will issue in the redemption of the body (v. 23), which in this context must be understood as part of the redemption of the whole creation. Creation will not be abandoned, but the work of Christ will be to take it on to its perfection, that perfection to which it points but which it cannot attain of itself.

Along with this we should take the idea that Christ has brought about the reconciliation of all things *(ta panta)* "through the blood of his cross" (Col. 1:20). The use of the concept of reconciliation rather than that of birth pangs seems to imply the overcoming of a hostility; creation is conceived of as not only fallen but in some way opposed to God.[10] Of course anything that resists the purposes of God must be thought of as in some sense hostile to him, and a fallen creation, thrown into disorder by the entrance of sin, certainly fits into this category. Paul is saying that whatever was wrong in the created order has now been put right by Christ's atoning

9. Frances Young regards the reference to the death of Christ here as "a clear sign that the judgment had begun; the tribulations and woes, the sufferings and pains, were initiated by his submission to death. . . . The final judgment had begun" (*Can These Dry Bones Live?* [London, 1982], p. 52). This view sees Christ as initiating the birth pangs by his death. But I am not sure that this takes sufficient notice of "was subjected" (v. 20; most understand this as a reference to Gen. 3:17-19) or of the whole creation as groaning and travailing "until now" (v. 22). Paul does not appear to be saying that creation entered into its groaning and travailing when Christ died, but that it has been doing this since the Fall.

10. Cf. F. F. Bruce, "here it is not simply subjection to futility but positive hostility that is implied on the part of the created universe. The universe has been involved in conflict with its Creator, and needs to be reconciled to him: the conflict must be replaced by peace. This peace has been made through Christ, by the shedding of his life-blood on the cross" (*The Epistles to the Colossians, to Philemon, and to the Ephesians* [Grand Rapids, 1984], pp. 74f.).

work.[11] Ralph Martin thinks that he "is intent on rebutting any idea that part of the universe is outside the scope of Christ's reconciling work."[12] Such an idea is monstrous. In his grand idea of the atonement Paul sees its effects as felt throughout the entire universe.

NON-PHYSICAL FRUSTRATION

There is then frustration that we share with the whole universe in which we live. But there is also a large amount of frustration that runs through human life which does not appear to have much relevance to the physical. Some of it is like the dilemma of the medical person in a Third World country in which there is not enough food. Confronted with a seriously ill patient, he knows that if he cures the patient someone else will die, for there is not enough food for all. He can scarcely refuse to exercise his healing skills, but there is a frustration in such a situation.

There is frustration in food-producing countries. If the wheat farmer, for example, does not produce all the food he can and sell it cheaply, people will die, for there is not enough food for all and many who need it have little money. But the way markets are, if he sells it cheaply he goes bankrupt and there is so much less food for sale. At the present moment there are problems with the huge surpluses some nations have accumulated. If they do not get them to the starving, people will die. If they simply pass them over to the places where they are needed, they will run local food producers out of business and less food will be produced in such lands.

11. E. Lohse comments, "The universe has been reconciled in that heaven and earth have been brought back into their divinely created and determined order through the resurrection and exaltation of Christ" (*Colossians and Philemon* [Philadelphia, 1971], p. 59). He says further that the reference to "the blood of his cross" "gives a new direction to the train of thought. A 'theology of glory,' which might view the consummation as already achieved, is corrected by the 'theology of the cross'" (*ibid.*, p. 60).

12. Ralph P. Martin, *Colossians and Philemon* (London, 1974), p. 60.

Nobody can deny that the distribution of food is in a mess, but how to solve the problem is not at all obvious. More frustration.

Frustration is part of political life. If the statesman arms his nation, all the experience of the past warns him that sooner or later those arms will be used; he is getting ready for war. If he does not arm his nation while others are arming theirs, his nation will be weak and will fall prey to some strong enemy. In Western lands democracy has evolved in many nations, often after hard struggles, and it never occurs to those who know democratic freedom that any other form of government can be compared to it. So the West has tried to install democracy wherever it has had the necessary influence, only to find that democracy rarely succeeds in Third World countries. The best-intentioned endeavours have a dreadful way of ending up in dictatorships.

Special mention should be made of the frustration felt by youth the world over. Young people everywhere feel that their elders have made a mess of society. And as one of the aged I say, With good reason. But when youth does get a chance, it mostly does no better than the aged. How can it? The system was produced by people who were young themselves once. But this is not a consideration that appeals to the young. So in large numbers they opt out of society. They evolve a subculture of their own, embodying values which society at large rejects. This is frustrating for both. The old would like to build a bridge to the young and do not know how to do this. The young can be furious with and contemptuous of the aged, who are so blind to real values as they see them. With few exceptions neither generation is particularly sympathetic to the other, and the scope for frustration is enormous.

Another frustration connected with age arises from the fact that the aged have learned much about life and the way to achieve worthwhile goals but physical frailty prevents them from putting much of it into practice. The young have boundless energy but have not yet acquired the experience that would tell them how best to use that energy. Frustration is part of life, and that at both ends of the normal life span.

Does Paul have something of this widespread frustration in

mind when he tells the Corinthians, in the words of Psalm 94:11, "The Lord knows the thoughts of the wise, that they are futile" (1 Cor. 3:20)? Our text of the Psalm refers to the thoughts "of man", not "of the wise"; it is uncertain whether Paul is quoting from a manuscript not extant or whether he is applying something that is said of all men to one class of men, the wise, in order to make his point that no matter which branch of the race is in mind, futility is characteristic of its thinking.[13] We are not to hold, for example, that the simple and uneducated are constantly frustrated by their inability to surmount obstacles while the more intelligent and the better informed cope with life with ease. It is part of life's futility that the best-laid schemes of the wisest of people so often end nowhere. It does not matter how great the man or how highly he is esteemed by his fellows, in the end his wisdom is no more than futile so long as it is purely earthly. Unless a person comes to see that Christ is the wisdom of God (1 Cor. 1:24), he is bound to lack true wisdom. It is true that we can get nowhere without our minds, but if we have only our minds it is also true that we can get nowhere in spiritual matters.

Paul is making the point that it is important to be humble before God and to receive his revelation as the true wisdom. Calvin considers this "an excellent passage for bringing down the confidence of the flesh, for here God declares from above that whatever the mind of man conceives and purposes is simply nothingness."[14] The modern world is almost a classic illustration of what Paul is saying. There have surely been few if any occasions

---

13. Robertson and Plummer point out that the Psalm "contrasts the designs of men with the designs of God, and therefore the idea of *sophos* is in the context" (A. Robertson and A. Plummer, *A Critical and Exegetical Commentary on the First Epistle of St Paul to the Corinthians* [Edinburgh, 1929], p. 71).

14. John Calvin, *The First Epistle of Paul the Apostle to the Corinthians*, trans. John W. Fraser (Grand Rapids, 1979), p. 81. Charles R. Erdman remarks that the reference "is to the emptiness, the vanity, of human wisdom, not merely as to its result but as to its very essence" (*The First Epistle of Paul to the Corinthians* [Philadelphia, 1966], p. 52).

when there have been so many brilliant thinkers in so many univer-
sities and other centres of learning. There can never have been a
time when technical achievement could match that of our age.
There has never been a period when it was possible to convey so
much information to so many in so short a time. And instead of all
this leading to a perfect world it leads to chaos and division and (to
use Paul's word) futility.

The biblical writers sometimes refer to idolatry as an outstand-
ing exercise in futility (e.g., Jer. 18:15; 51:17-18; cf. Isa. 2:20; Acts
14:15), and there are passages that pour scorn on it (e.g., Isa.
44:9ff.). It is so obviously a futile proceeding to worship a god our
own hands have made that we rarely give more than passing heed
to such passages. But we should not overlook the fact that the
manufacture of idols is a flourishing industry, none the less so because our idols tend to be more sophisticated than images of wood
and stone. Thus we may make an idol of communism or humanism
or materialism. Some of us worship success, our home, our business, popularity, social climbing, or comfort. Someone has said
that the greatest modern idol has the shape of a mushroom cloud.
Our idols are many and varied, and they have this in common, that
it is futile to offer to any of them the devotion, the time, and the
energy that they demand. In the end the idolater loses everything.
Joy Davidman says, "The real horror of idols is not merely that
they give us nothing, but that they take away from us even that
which we have." She has just said, with reference to those whose
god is the home, the office, and entertainment: "The house devours
the housewife, the office rots the executive with ulcers, and canned
entertainments leave us incapable of entertaining ourselves. Have
our idols done us no harm?"[15]

Paul, of course, implies that there is a way out of futility, as he
has made clear in his explanation of the significance of the cross.
The preaching of the cross, Paul has said, "is folly to those who are
perishing" (1 Cor. 1:18), and he has dismissed the wisdom of the
wise and the understanding of the intelligent as made nothing

15. Joy Davidman, *Smoke on the Mountain* (London, 1957), pp. 38f.

before God. In that situation God in his wisdom provided that the world's wisdom would not give knowledge of him, but that "through the folly of the preached message" God would save believers (1 Cor. 1:21). So it is that he lays down his apostolic procedure: "*We* preach Christ crucified" (1 Cor. 1:23). His *we* is emphatic: whatever be the case with others, *we* apostles and indeed *we* Christians proclaim the cross. It is this that overcomes the futility of the world's thinking.

The truth that the world's thinking is futile comes before us again in Ephesians 4:17-18: "This therefore I say and testify in the Lord, that you no longer walk as also the Gentiles walk, in the futility of their mind, being darkened in understanding, alienated from the life of God through the ignorance that is in them on account of the hardening of their heart. . . ." Once more we have the thought that those outside Christ are futile in their thinking. Being alienated from God and having darkness within them, they cannot but be darkened in their understanding and quite unable to think clearly. We should be clear that it is the best in the pagan world that is in mind, not the worst: "The very strong noun 'futility' implies emptiness, idleness, vanity, foolishness, purposelessness, and frustration. With one single word Paul describes the majority of the inhabitants of the Greco-Roman empire, including the shapers and beneficiaries of its magnificent cultural elements, as aiming with silly methods at a meaningless goal!"[16] It is frustrating in the extreme when the best endeavours of the best-intentioned people must be categorized in this way. But if we are to take the biblical revelation seriously, that is indeed the case.

16. Markus Barth, *Ephesians*, II (New York, 1960), p. 499. He later says that the New Testament authors "wanted to say that in the light of the greatness of God's gift, even man's greatest possessions, capacities, and performances, including those of the cultured Greeks and the uncounted 'noble savages,' lose their glory", and further, "The Jews are as much under God's wrath as are the Gentiles" (*ibid.*, p. 529). T. K. Abbott also sees a reference to "the whole moral and intellectual character of heathenism; their powers were wasted without fruit" (*A Critical and Exegetical Commentary on the Epistles to the Ephesians and to the Colossians* [Edinburgh, 1953], p. 129).

Charles Hodge sees in the word translated "futility" a reference to "moral as well as intellectual worthlessness, or fatuity" and goes on to say that everything "in the following verses respecting the blindness and depravity of the heathen" is comprehended in the word.[17] We are not to think of an intellectual process only; futility does indeed characterize the thinking of the people in question, but it extends also to their manner of living.

This perhaps becomes a little clearer if we reflect on the point Paul makes in the opening of his letter to the Romans. Here he tells his readers of people who "having known God, did not glorify him as God or give him thanks, but were made futile in their thoughts and their foolish heart was darkened" (Rom. 1:21). The thought is that when people wilfully reject the knowledge of God they take the meaning out of life. If we see a great God who has created everything and who is working out a purpose such that every person he has made has a place in that purpose and therefore has something useful and worthwhile to do, then the whole of life is meaningful. But if we reject the knowledge of God, then what is our answer to the question that inevitably arises sometime in our life: "What's the point of it all?" There seems to be no answer because there is no point in a pointless existence. And if there is no answer, another question arises, "What does it matter what I do?" Since no answer can be given to that either in a world without God, then one might as well give oneself over to securing what pleasure one can by whatever means there are at one's disposal. Morality goes out the window together with meaning. The tragedy of much modern life is that the abandonment of the knowledge of God means that futility has taken over.[18]

Paul argues that Christians are not in the same case as the godless. He uses an emphatic *you* when he says, "But *you* did not so learn Christ", and he categorizes the Christian life as the result of

17. Charles Hodge, *A Commentary on the Epistle to the Ephesians* (repr. London, 1964), pp. 250f.

18. C. Leslie Mitton makes much of this point in his New Century Bible Commentary, *Ephesians* (London and Grand Rapids, 1981), p. 159.

an act of divine creativity (Eph. 4:20-24). We do not have here an explicit reference to the cross, but there can be little doubt that it is in mind. The "old man" is not done away, nor is the "new man" brought into being apart from Christ's saving work. That saving work has among other things done away with the futility that otherwise covered so much in life.

REDEMPTION FROM A FUTILE LIFE

Peter calls on his correspondents to pass their lives in fear (or reverence), "knowing that not with corruptible things, with silver or gold, were you redeemed from your futile way of life handed down from the fathers" (1 Pet. 1:18). The futile life-style was clearly the one that heathen forefathers had passed on to them—a life-style that featured the worship of idols. These are often categorized in the Greek translation of the Old Testament with words from the word group Peter uses here (e.g., Lev. 17:7; Jer. 8:19; cf. Acts 14:15). Could anything be more obviously futile than worshipping gods made by the worshippers themselves? But Peter is concerned not with the act of worship alone but with the whole life-style to which such worship led. It is the same thought that we have seen before: it is impossible to separate one part of life from another as though we live in watertight compartments. There is a unity in life, a wholeness, and if our worship is futile, then so is all else. Hort remarks on the futility in question here: "Its vanity consists in its essential unreality and want of correspondence to the truth of things, its inability to fulfil the promises which it suggests, and its universal unproductiveness."[19] It fits in with what we have seen about futility elsewhere.

Peter, of course, is not so much concerned with what that futility had been like as with deliverance from it, but it is interesting that he uses this strong word to characterize it. It had been an

19. F. J. A. Hort, *The First Epistle of St Peter I.1 II.17* (London, 1898), p. 75.

unsatisfying and unsatisfactory life.[20] But Peter is concerned with the way they have been freed from it. He is speaking of Christ's death on the cross, for he goes on to refer to Christ's "precious blood, as of a lamb without blemish and without spot" (v. 19), and, of course, his verb "redeemed" points to the same thing. The fundamental idea in redemption is the payment of a price, which may be for the release of a prisoner of war or of a slave, or for the restoration to its rightful owner of land or some other possession that has been sold in a time of financial stringency. The important thing is the payment of a price. Cranfield points out that the context makes it clear that the passage is not to be understood in the sense "you were delivered". There are references to money, to the blood of Christ, and to sacrifice, and he further thinks that Jesus' ransom saying (Mark 10:45) may be in Peter's mind.[21] We must take seriously the idea that a price was paid to deliver people from their futility. The word group may be used metaphorically, but it is the idea of price or cost that gives it its point. Peter then is saying that Christ paid the price to buy the people of whom he is speaking out of their whole way of life. Futility cannot stand before such an atoning act as the death of Christ. Put another way, if Christ paid such a price, then it is nonsense to say that those for whom he paid it live only futile lives. Clearly he has bought them out of futility and given them a life that is meaningful.

Sometimes we are warned about a particular area of futility, one which is concerned with speech. Thus Titus is urged to avoid foolish discussions, genealogies, dissensions, and legal controversies (Tit. 3:9), which are described as "profitless and futile" (interestingly the false teachers are said to utter "bombastic words of futility" [2 Pet. 2:18]). There is dispute as to the precise meaning

20. Cf. Alan M. Stibbs: the way of life in question "lacked reverence for the true God and, in consequence, it lacked a proper regard for real values. It produced no worthwhile result. It was wholly determined by inherited usage, by tradition and convention" (*The First Epistle General of Peter* [London, 1959], p. 90).

21. C. E. B. Cranfield, *The First Epistle of Peter* (London, 1950), p. 39.

of some of these terms,[22] but the general thrust of the exhortation is clear. We are all aware of the ease with which we can slip into unnecessary discussions of things that do not matter; we can spend our lives engaging in empty talk and pursuing objects of no real value. We are being warned against this. The salvation Christ died to bring is among other things a salvation from futility. It is ironical in the extreme when the saved are careless enough to live lives that can issue only in a renewed form of futility. In Titus foolish discussions are set in opposition to the good works to which "those who have believed God" are devoted. Faith in God leads to one sort of life, foolish discussions and the like to quite another. In saving us God has a purpose for us, and that purpose is concerned with solid achievement, not stupidity and emptiness.

FACT, NOT FICTION

It is possible to be self-deceived, even when we are promoting what we see as right. James warns that there can be futility in a highly religious person: "If anyone thinks he is religious and does not bridle his tongue but deceives his own heart, this man's religion is futile" (Jas. 1:26). Futility comes so easily to the human race that it is quite possible for someone to profess to be a Christian and in fact still to hold fast to futility. The particular example that James chooses is the person whose tongue is not under control, but what he says applies equally to anyone who "deceives his own heart". The essence of infidelity is putting self at the centre and ignoring the demands of God. There is always the temptation for those who profess the Christian way to put all their emphasis on the outward. They may convince themselves that their regular attendance at

22. Thus "genealogies" is often taken to refer to the endless Gnostic speculations about the celestial emanations with their extraordinary genealogical connections. But there is no evidence that any of these was as early as the letter to Titus, and it is better to see a reference to the subtleties of rabbinic speculation of the sort we find in the Book of Jubilees (so, e.g., Ronald A. Ward, *Commentary on 1 & 2 Timothy & Titus* [Waco, 1974], p. 29).

worship, their deep regard for observing saints' days and the like, their giving to good causes are essential Christianity. I do not, of course, belittle outward observances. In their place they are very important, for they can give outward expression to a deep inward reality and they can foster and build up that reality. But James is concerned with the person whose whole emphasis is on the outward. To see Christianity in this way is to engage in the final futility.

Paul draws attention to the importance of the connection between fact and faith. In his notable discussion of the resurrection in 1 Corinthians he stresses the significance of the fact that Christ did rise. If that did not happen, he says, "empty is our preaching, empty too is your faith"; and again, "if Christ has not been raised, futile is your faith, you are still in your sins" (1 Cor. 15:14, 17). An empty faith in a dead Christ would be useless. When he says that without the resurrection their faith would be "empty", he is saying that there would be nothing in it, it would lack real content. When he goes on to say that it would be "futile", he says it would be pointless, with no effect; in that case they would still be "in" their sins. Faith, in itself, does not remove sins. For forgiveness to take place something objective must happen; we cannot just talk ourselves or reason ourselves into being forgiven. As O. Bauernfeind puts it, "A faith orientated to a resurrection which did not take place in the field of history could not be regarded as a noteworthy or even a supreme religion."[23] A concern for right inner attitudes is legitimate, but if there is no more than this we are caught up in futility. There must be a factual basis for the central tenets of Christianity, and specifically for Christ's atoning death and resurrection, or the believer has been engaging in a futile pursuit. He has embraced a faith that is completely worthless, barren of results. He has occupied himself in an exercise of self-deception.

23. TDNT, IV, p. 522. A. Robertson and A. Plummer point out that there is often no great difference between the words here rendered "empty" and "futile", but here there is: "*kenē* is 'wanting in reality,' *mataia* 'wanting in result,' 'fruitless,' 'futile'" (*A Critical and Exegetical Commentary on the First Epistle of St Paul to the Corinthians* [Edinburgh, 1929], p. 349).

THE ANSWER TO FUTILITY

THE "NOW" AND THE "NOT YET"

The writer to the Hebrews quotes from Psalm 8:4-6 to bring out something of the dignity God accords the human race. He has made man a little lower than the angels, the Psalmist says, crowned him with glory and honour, and he has subjected all things under his feet (Heb. 2:6-8). It is a most significant place for any created being to occupy. The writer goes on to notice that nothing is omitted from that subjection: everything is included. Then he proceeds to point out that that is not the way it is: "But now not yet do we see all things subjected to him." Every one of us experiences this. As I have written elsewhere: "The full promise of the psalm awaits realization. It is part of the frustration of life that in every part of it there are the equivalents of the 'thorns and thistles' (Gen. 3:18) that make life so hard for the tiller of the soil. Everyone knows what it is to chafe under the limitations under which he must do his work while he glimpses the vision of what would be possible were it not for those cramping limitations."[24] Frustration is part of life as we know it.

But our author does not stop there. He goes on, "But we see Jesus, who was made a little lower than angels" and, because he suffered death, is "now crowned with glory and honour" (Heb. 2:9). In other words, though we on earth suffer frustration, we know that Christ has come and died for us and thus has brought about the fulfilment of the Psalm. The answer to our frustrations is in the cross. We may not know the answer, for there is a "not yet" to which we must give attention. But when we look at the cross, we know that there is an answer and that the death of our Saviour is instrumental in bringing it about.

In one way or another Christians have, of course, seen something of the defeat of frustration. Obviously it would not be true to say that believers have universally lived without feeling frustrated and without sensing the futility of much of the human experience. Christians live in the same world as nonbelievers and share many

24 Frank E. Gaebelein, ed., *The Expositor's Bible Commentary*, vol. 12 (Hebrews-Revelation) (Grand Rapids, 1981), p. 25.

of the same experiences. But it is also true that Christians who are in earnest about living out their faith rarely if ever find life futile. May I point to the large number of young men and women (and these days older ones, too) who have found fulfilment in serving in the world's mission fields. They almost invariably find themselves without many of the comforts and conveniences that they had taken for granted back home and without which many of their contemporaries would find life intolerable. They have been the butt of the ridicule of a generation which has managed to turn the expression 'do-gooder' into a term of abuse. They have often found that they have received no welcome from those to whom they have brought the message of God's gift of eternal life. They mostly find it very difficult indeed to bring any significant number of people to confess Christ. They come across new frustrations, for example, when they bring the latest in medical help only to find that the people among whom they live prefer to go to the witch doctors, or when they cannot persuade them to practise the elementary rules of hygiene that would certainly reduce disease, or when they find the hard heads among whom they live opting for the 'practical' business of learning how to hunt and fish instead of allowing children to give years over to education. But through it all they have been ridiculously happy and have experienced wonderfully fulfilling lives.

I mention missionaries as being obvious examples of people in whom Christ's defeat of futility and frustration is to be seen, but that same victory is apparent in ever so many humble and ordinary Christians serving Christ quietly in their lowly places. The defeat of futility is a wonderful part of being Christian.

With Christians throughout the ages we must say that the death of Christ has dealt with the problem of our sins. Christ has paid our penalty. Christ has shown us the love of God in such a way that we cannot but respond with an answering love that affects all our living. Christ has won the victory over all the forces of death and hell and evil.

But we must also say that Christ has redeemed us from futility and frustration.

CHAPTER FOUR

The Answer to Ignorance

For many modern humanists ignorance is the prime enemy of the human race. With a touching faith in the possibilities in fallen human nature they press on with their goal of bringing a greater degree of education to a greater number of people. Now I do not wish it to be thought that I have any objection to the widest possible spread of education. For most of my adult life (and for that matter my life as a child as well) I have been involved in education in one way or another, and I am a fervent believer in the importance of raising educational standards worldwide. There is little hope for any nation or people, developed or underdeveloped, unless the population as a whole is educated. Education liberates minds and opens the way to an enrichment of life. Education looses people from a variety of superstitions (though we should not overlook the fact that many well-educated people are curiously superstitious). Education gives people the knowledge and the skills they need to fashion for themselves a better standard of living in a technological age. Education opens the door so that very ordinary people may have access to the thinking of the great ones through the ages as that thinking is recorded in the books they have left. Education enables us to read the Bible, the word of God to us, and to know more of his love and more of our duty to him. Education enables us to come to grips with the thoughts of great Christians in every age and thus to enlarge our understanding of the Christian life. I am happy at every evidence of the progress of education in the community in which I live and at what I hear of its advances in other places. I am glad that when Christian missionaries go forth with the gospel they so often are very much to the fore in raising educational standards in the lands to which they go.

It is not education to which I object, but the simple faith that education of itself provides the answers to our problems. This generation as much as any other needs to learn that an educated devil is no improvement on an uneducated devil. If the heart remains deceitful and desperately wicked (Jer. 17:9), then all the knowledge the mind may pick up is not going to lead to utopia. We must not put our trust in education, still less in the secular-style education common in so many parts of our world which more or less politely ushers God out of his creation.

An interesting possibility arises from a suggestion of Bishop Montefiore, that perhaps our brains are too big for us to manage them successfully: "One cannot help wondering whether the brain of man is not in some ways similar to the horns of the Irish elk, grown too large to be useful—or rather, grown so large that it will be man's undoing unless he learns to control its use. The history of mankind shows how twisted man is, suffering as theologians say from original sin, and with a tendency to quarrel and to fight and to use his gifts for his own aggrandisement without much thought either for his fellowmen, or for his fellow members of the animal kingdom."[1] I do not see how it can be seriously disputed that our intellectual capacity has outgrown our moral sense: we are much better at devising intricate ways of attaining the ends we have chosen for what we see as our own advantage than we are at doing what we recognize as the right thing. Our science and technology have given us the means of producing many wonderful things (just look around your kitchen!). And we use our knowledge to threaten the very existence of the race with our atomic toys. We have the ability to land men on the moon but we allow millions of our fellow earth-dwellers to die of starvation. Clearly our brains are such

1. Hugh Montefiore, *The Probability of God* (London, 1985), p. 105.

that they are already bringing about the destruction of significant numbers of the species, and they have brought about a situation in which it is quite possible that in the not too distant future we will destroy the rest. Our problem is not that we do not have the capacity, by the grace of God, to do our duty to God and our fellows. It is rather that we are so interested in what we can do for our selfish interests that, as a race, we do not care what our duty to God and our fellows is. We so easily slip into doing evil.

SINS DONE IN IGNORANCE

The Old Testament writers were clear that it is possible to sin in ignorance and that, while this is not as bad as wilful defiance of God, it is serious enough to demand that something be done about it. The Levitical system provided that there be sacrifices for sins of inadvertence (e.g., Lev. 4:2, 13, 22, 27; 5:14), and the very existence of the Day of Atonement makes it clear that there were sins for which no sacrifice had been offered, evidently including sins which people had not recognized at the time they committed them. But sin is sin even if one does not realize it at the time of the action, and the whole thrust of Old Testament teaching is that even sins done in ignorance matter. They must be atoned if one is to be at peace with God.

It seems to be the presumption of the New Testament writers that, if we really understood what sin is and what consequences it inevitably brings, we would flee from it instead of embracing it as we so frequently do. For that reason they can link sin with ignorance. Thus Peter can write of "the lusts formerly (practised) in your ignorance" (1 Pet. 1:14). Commentators sometimes argue as to whether this points to Gentile or Jewish readers, but surely this is to miss the point. It applies to both groups. Before they came to know Christ they were both ruled by lusts of various kinds, which no longer have sway over them. In Christ they have learned to know better, and that, of course, is the point Peter is making. It is probably this kind of sin that is in mind when the writer to the

Hebrews speaks of the high priest as dealing gently with "the ignorant and straying ones" (Heb. 5:2)[2] and when he says that on the Day of Atonement the high priest made an offering "for himself and the ignorances of the people" (Heb. 9:7).[3]

Paul can speak of people who were "alienated from the life of God on account of the ignorance that is in them" (Eph. 4:18).[4] This takes a somewhat different view of sin, but again ascribes it to ignorance. Would anyone who really understood what he was doing genuinely choose to live in opposition to God? The very idea is preposterous, but Paul knew of people who lived that way and the church has encountered them in their millions throughout the centuries. The only possible conclusion is that they did not (and do not) know what they were (and are) doing. We should notice further that the passage goes on to speak of the hardening of the hearts of these ignorant people and then of their being past feeling and giving themselves up "to lasciviousness, in order to work all manner of uncleanness in covetousness". The ignorance of which the writer speaks does not remain an innocent ignorance. Ignorance has a habit of progressing in evil; it leads from one sin to another. Why not? It lacks the knowledge that would save it from such a degeneration.

We must bear in mind that there are different kinds of ig-

2. P. E. Hughes explains this: "those who have sinned whether through offending in ignorance of the divine law or through wandering away from the path of the will of God which has been set before them. The perversity of the human heart is such that, even if it should be possible for a person to be free from sins of waywardness, yet no man can claim to be free from sins of ignorance or inadvertency" (A Commentary on the Epistle to the Hebrews [Grand Rapids, 1979], p. 178).

3. The Rabbis were clear that the Day of Atonement did not atone for deliberate sins. In the Mishnah we read, "If a man said, 'I will sin and repent, and sin again and repent', he will be given no chance to repent. [If he said,] 'I will sin and the Day of Atonement will effect atonement', then the Day of Atonement effects no atonement" (Yoma 8:9, Danby's translation).

4. Lloyd-Jones remarks that "All our troubles ultimately emanate from our ignorance of God. That is the real trouble in the world today" (D. Martyn Lloyd-Jones, The Cross [Eastbourne, 1986], p. 72).

norance. Paul could claim that in the days when he persecuted the church he was in fact "a blasphemer and a persecutor and insolent", but he obtained mercy, he says, "because I did it in unbelief, being ignorant" (1 Tim. 1:13). He does not regard such a sin as one that did not matter. He still needed forgiveness, and he rejoices that he has received that forgiveness. What he had done had been wrong, but Paul had repented and been forgiven for that wrong.

But there were other sins done in ignorance which may not have been forgiven. The crucifixion of Jesus was a sin done in ignorance. Jesus prayed for his executioners, "Father, forgive them, for they do not know what they are doing" (Luke 23:34). Though they did not understand that they were putting to death the very Son of God, they were yet committing a very serious sin. It was not to be thought that it would be dismissed lightly, as something that did not matter. Were they ever forgiven? We do not know. We know only that their ignorance did not mean that they were guiltless. We get a similar thought in Acts, where we are told that the crucifixion was done in ignorance (Acts 3:17) and almost immediately there is a call for repentance (v. 19). This time it is not Gentile soldiers whose ignorance is in mind but Jewish people, those who had the revelation in the Old Testament and who stood in a special relationship to God. The point is that their ignorance is culpable. Peter's hearers could have known better. They had had Jesus live and move among them, and they should have come to know that he was the Son of God and our Saviour. There had been men and women who saw and heard Jesus and who believed in him and followed him. Those who killed him were thus not to be excused. Ernst Haenchen maintains that "the real guilt lies precisely in the *agnoia*: if men had not hardened their heart against God, they would have recognised Jesus. Only so does it become plain that in the Cross our guilt is revealed."[5] So far from their ignorance

5. Ernst Haenchen, *The Acts of the Apostles* (Oxford, 1971), p. 207, n. 4. BAGD defines the word *agnoia* as "ignorance", but also says, "esp. in religious sense, almost = sin".

being an excuse for their sin it was the cause of their guilt. They could have known better. They were in darkness only because they had rejected the light.

People may wilfully forget the activities of God (2 Pet. 3:5), and they may twist[6] the Scriptures to their own destruction (2 Pet. 3:16). It is not that it is impossible to understand the Scriptures. Granted that there are some difficult passages, it is also the case that perfectly ordinary people, with no more than the usual quota of brains (and sometimes with much less than the average), can read Scripture to their profit. They find the essential message to be clear and helpful. As this is so obviously possible, it is blameworthy when people twist the words to make them mean something quite different.

There is a somewhat different way of sinning when people sin wilfully after receiving the knowledge of the truth (Heb. 10:26). This shows clearly that sin is not always a matter of ignorance, and further that for this reason salvation is not infallibly guaranteed by a recognition of truth. It is possible to look truth in the face and reject it. When Peter speaks of muzzling the ignorance of foolish men (1 Pet. 2:15) it seems that it is this sort of ignorance he has in mind, even though the foolish people in question had not had the blessing of instruction in the Christian way. But Christians were being vigorously opposed by people who ought to have known better. Clearly the Christians to whom he writes were being slandered and opposed by those he calls "foolish" and whose opposition he puts down to "ignorance". But equally clearly he does not regard that ignorance as blameless. These opponents of the Christian way

6. The verb *strebloō* is used of twisting or straining tight, of the action of windlasses, screwing up the strings of an instrument, twisting a dislocated limb with a view to setting it. It is used also of wrestlers who presumably twisted for a very different reason. The verb is used of twisting in torture (LSJ). Michael Green comments, "a delightful word, *strebloō*, meaning literally 'tighten with a windlass'" (*The Second Epistle General of Peter and the General Epistle of Jude* [London, 1968], p. 146).

are guilty and are to be put to silence.[7] In the here and now this is to be done by the good lives of believers.

People of course may be confronted with the truth without recognizing it for what it is. This may take place because they are so firmly entrenched in traditional ways of thinking and living that they will not open their minds to the new thing that God is saying. That is what Paul has in mind when he speaks of those who are ignorant of "the righteousness of God" and who "seek to establish their own righteousness" (Rom. 10:3). They were so sure that they were right that they did not sufficiently examine the revelation that God made and which might have delivered them from their error. Paul says they did not subject themselves to God's righteousness, so that their culpable ignorance led them to disobedience.

KNOWLEDGE AND SALVATION

Ignorance, then, may at times mitigate an offence and at times be culpable in itself and thus the very cause of sin. The other side of this coin is the fact that in the New Testament salvation is often connected with knowledge in some way. We should not understand this as though Christianity were a form of Gnosticism or intellectualism, putting its major emphasis on some form of knowledge accessible only to the privileged initiates. The opposite is the case.

7. F. W. Beare distinguishes between *agnoia* (1:14) and *agnōsia* (here). The former "is used of the ignorance which is a mere lack of knowledge, which is therefore pardonable and may be overlooked. . . . *agnōsia* on the other hand means culpable ignorance, the ignorance that shuts out and rejects knowledge which is offered; thus it involves moral delinquency. Here the thought is of such ignorance venting itself in slander of the good" (*The First Epistle of Peter* [Oxford, 1947], p. 117). Beare also draws attention to the Greek translation of Prov. 1:22 for an explanation of "foolish": "Fools, having their hearts set upon insolence, show themselves impious and hate discernment." J. N. D. Kelly sees this latter word as a description of "the arrogant unbeliever who sets himself up against truth and right" (*A Commentary on the Epistles of Peter and of Jude* [London, 1969], p. 111).

Christianity repudiates vigorously any suggestion that it is knowledge as such that matters or that this knowledge is open only to a privileged circle. The knowledge that matters so much to the New Testament writers is the knowledge that takes away the kind of ignorance of which we have been speaking. It is a knowledge that gives the chief place to God, for what matters is not that we know him but that "the Lord knows those that are his" (2 Tim. 2:19). Paul can begin to speak of knowing God and switch in midstream to bring out the more important truth: "and now, having known God, or rather having been known by God . . ." (Gal. 4:9). Our knowledge matters little; it is God's knowledge, and specifically his knowledge of us, that matters, for when he knows us as his people we are saved indeed. Sometimes it is his foreknowledge that is brought out (e.g., Rom. 8:29; 11:2). It gives assurance to believers to reflect that "God is greater than our heart and knows all things" (1 John 3:20). Jesus can speak of knowing those who belong to him and proceed to connect this with his saving death; he says, "I am the Good Shepherd and know my own . . . and I lay down my life for the sheep" (John 10:14-15).

Salvation is connected with knowing God. It was to be the function of John the Baptist "to give the knowledge of salvation to his people in the forgiveness of their sins" (Luke 1:77). Those who live in lustful passions may be described as "the Gentiles who do not know God" (1 Thess. 4:5). This does not, of course, mean those Gentiles who do not know God in contrast to others who do, for to the apostle all the Gentiles came under this condemnation.[8] Ignorance alienates people from "the life of God" (Eph. 4:18), and again Paul can call on people in these terms: "Wake up righteously and stop sinning, for some have ignorance of God" (1 Cor. 15:34). Once more sin is located in ignorance, and this time the im-

8. Ernest Best comments, "If the Jew is characterized by the fact that God has made himself known to him, the pagan is characterised by his failure to know God—and the inevitable result is sin, here particularized as 'lustful passion'" (*A Commentary on the First and Second Epistles to the Thessalonians* [London, 1977], p. 165).

plication is that salvation means waking up out of that ignorance and thus into the knowledge of God.[9]

Just as the sinful person is here characterized as ignorant, so elsewhere in the same letter Paul can speak of the believer as "you who have knowledge" (1 Cor. 8:10). Or he may say that God "makes known the riches of his glory" (Rom. 9:23). Peter calls on "all the house of Israel" to know what God has done in Christ (Acts 2:36). Perhaps the most far-reaching statement about knowledge is that in which Jesus includes in his prayer the words: "This is life eternal, that they may know you, the only true God, and him whom you sent, Jesus Christ" (John 17:3). Eternal life is not simply life that goes on and on. Life without end might conceivably mean misery without end, which, of course, is the traditional understanding of hell. Eternal life is life of a particular quality; it means going on and on in the knowledge of God.[10] The mention of Jesus Christ does not mean two separate pieces of knowledge as though the two were different so that it would be possible to know the one without knowing the other. This is alien to the thought of the passage. It is one knowledge of one God, manifested in Jesus Christ, that is meant.[11] Elsewhere we find that love and the knowledge of

9. R. Bultmann sees Stoic influence behind this and a few other passages and goes on, "Early Christianity could accept this usage to the extent that it expresses the destiny of the world's alienation from God, its fallen estate, and its dependence upon revelation. . . . But the Christian usage is naturally not the same as the Gnostic, since the ideas of sin and grace are very different" (TDNT, I, p. 119). The word for "ignorance", *agnōsia,* means ignorance "not predominantly in the intellectual sense, but . . . a lack of religious experience or *lack of spiritual discernment*" (BAGD).

10. J. I. Packer has written a whole book called *Knowing God* (London, 1973). He says, "The conviction behind the book is that ignorance of God . . . lies at the root of much of the church's weakness today" (p. 6). He says further, "What were we made for? To know God. What aim should we set ourselves in life? To know God. What is the 'eternal life' that Jesus gives? Knowledge of God" (p. 29).

11. "It is one faith in God and one knowledge of Him, by which the knowledge of God in the Old Testament (Deut. vi.4) is fulfilled, and which is

God go together, for we read that "everyone who loves has been begotten of God and knows God" (1 John 4:7; the converse immediately follows, "he who does not love does not know God"). John is not here laying a duty on his readers as though he were saying, "everyone who has been begotten of God must love". He is drawing attention to the origin of Christian life in the love of God and to the fact that that love of God awakes an answering love in the believer. Christian love is always an answering love, a response to the love of God that has sought us out. In the words of the old hymn, it is "Loving him who first loved me." And such a love carries with it the consequence that the believer knows God, too.[12] To know the creative love of God is to know God.

It is significant that the New Testament writers speak often of witness, for this points to facts that ought to be known. The risen Jesus told his followers that they were to be his "witnesses" to the very end of the earth (Acts 1:8), and Peter speaks of the function of the apostle as that of witness to Christ's resurrection (Acts 1:22), while he himself is a witness of Christ's sufferings (1 Pet. 5:1). John writes, "And this is the testimony, that God has given us life eternal, and this life is in his Son" (1 John 5:11). Examples could be multiplied, especially in the Johannine writings. Wherever witness is referred to, it is plain that God has acted in Christ for salvation and that the function of Christians is to testify so that people will come into knowledge for themselves.

---

set against the ignorance of Jew (viii.55) and Gentile alike. Faith in Jesus Christ as The Apostle of the Father—*him whom thou didst send*—is the ground of the Christian knowledge of God, and this true and full knowledge of God is the ground of eternal life" (E. C. Hoskyns, *The Fourth Gospel* [London, 1950], p. 498).

12. John is not saying that non-Christians cannot love one another. They can, of course, and sometimes their love for one another puts Christians to shame. John is writing about *agapē*, the love that is to be seen in the cross (1 John 4:10), and which is characteristically a love for the unworthy. This love in God awakens an answering love in believers, a love for God and for other people, a love independent of merit or attractiveness in the beloved. This love responding to God's love is not found in unbelievers.

Salvation and knowledge are connected in a variety of ways. Thus salvation comes pretty close to being the knowledge of truth, for God wills that "all men be saved and come into knowledge of truth" (1 Tim. 2:4);[13] Christians are those who "believe and know the truth" (1 Tim. 4:3). Unbelievers, by the same token, are those who, despite the fact that they are always learning, "are never able to come to the knowledge of truth" (2 Tim. 3:7). These unbelievers are not unlike those whom "the god of this age has blinded" and prevented from seeing "the light of the gospel of the glory of Christ" (2 Cor. 4:4). In the opening of 2 John the church at large is described as "all those who know the truth" (2 John 1). Clearly the early Christians saw truth as very important, so important that to know it is the one essential thing. This is not something different from knowing God, for the truth in question is the truth that God has revealed. We must bear in mind that truth is connected with Christ, who is the truth (John 14:6), and that "truth is in Jesus" (Eph. 4:21). The gospel is "the word of truth" (Eph. 1:13; cf. "the word of the truth of the gospel" [Col. 1:5]); thus Paul can write of "the truth of the gospel" (Gal. 2:5). The Holy Spirit is "the Spirit of truth" (John 14:17; 15:26; 16:13), and Christians are those who are "of the truth" (1 John 3:19). We must bear in mind the tremendous emphasis the New Testament places on truth when we are thinking about the message the first Christians proclaimed. They were not setting forth some fine theory but bearing their witness to what they knew to be the truth.

But truth is not the only way the Christian message is characterized. Paul can speak of God as having made known "the riches of his glory" (Rom. 9:23), and as having made his light shine in our hearts and given us "the light of the knowledge of the glory of God in the face of Jesus Christ" (2 Cor. 4:6). Salvation of course is wrapped up in Christ and his atoning sacrifice, so it is significant

---

13. Cf. J. N. D. Kelly, "'Knowledge' includes not only rational apprehension on the believer's part, but also acceptance by faith, while 'truth' is the whole revelation of God in Christ" (*A Commentary on the Pastoral Epistles* [London, 1963], p. 62).

that Paul says, "I know whom I have believed" (2 Tim. 1:12), and
writes to the Corinthians, "you know the grace of our Lord Jesus
Christ" (2 Cor. 8:9), which may point to a similar saving
knowledge of Christ. It is not surprising that he values it so highly
that he can say, "I count all things loss for the sake of the excellen-
cy of the knowledge of Christ Jesus my Lord", and he goes on to
speak of having the righteousness that is "through faith in Christ"
(Phil. 3:8-9). He proceeds to speak of knowing Christ and the
power of his resurrection and the fellowship of his sufferings
(v. 10). Clearly Paul's understanding of Christian knowledge has a
strong link with the death and resurrection of Christ, a thought we
find again with his "knowing that Christ, having been raised from
the dead, dies no more" (Rom. 6:9). This knowledge of the Saviour
is given a certain emphasis in 2 Peter (1:8; 2:20; 3:18; knowledge
of Christ's power [1:16]), in which epistle it is clear that the
knowledge of Christ may be equated with salvation. In 1 John we
read, "We know that the Son of God has come and has given us an
understanding so that we know him that is true" (1 John 5:20);
knowledge is connected with the coming of the Son of God and the
work he has accomplished. Even more important, of course, is the
fact that Jesus says, "I am the Good Shepherd and know my own",
though he immediately adds, "and my own know me" (John
10:14). He goes on to say, "I lay down my life for the sheep"
(v. 15). Clearly knowledge and the saving act stand close together.

Sometimes the thought is rather that of knowing the Father
(1 John 2:14). There is a prayer that God, "the Father of glory, may
give you a spirit of wisdom and revelation in the knowledge of
him" (Eph. 1:17), and another that people may grow "in the
knowledge of God" (Col. 1:10). It is not clear whether it is knowing the Father or the Son in the references to knowing "him that is
from the beginning" (1 John 2:13) and to knowing "that we know
him" (1 John 2:3; perhaps John is not differentiating too sharply
between them at this point). But it is clear that this knowledge is of
the utmost importance. John is telling his readers how "we may
know that we know"; it is important to have assurance on this
point. This is a New Testament distinctive; it is not something we
should take for granted, for in the Old Testament it is rare to find

anyone claiming to know God. The prophets sometimes expressed the hope that people would come to this knowledge (cf. Jer. 31:34) and more often castigated their hearers for not knowing God (Isa. 1:3; Jer. 9:6; etc.). By contrast the New Testament writers insisted that the knowledge of God has been made possible by what Christ did and indeed that salvation may well be understood in terms of this knowledge. We see then that there is emphasis on knowing the truth and on knowing the way of God.

This may be put in the form "knowing that a man is not justified from works of law but through faith in Jesus Christ" (Gal. 2:16), for the manner of salvation is not by what human endeavour can accomplish, but by the grace of God in Christ. To know that works of law are unavailing, to know that it is what Christ has done that brings salvation, and thus to know that justification comes through faith in Christ is to be acceptable to God. Hans Dieter Betz points out that "The first word of v 16 states the basis for being a Christian in distinction from being a Jew. This basis is 'theological conviction' (*eidotes* ['we know']) over against birth (v 15)."[14] Perhaps this is a good place to point out that there is an intellectual aspect to faith, as the many New Testament references to "believing that—" show (e.g., John 8:24; 11:27; Rom. 10:9). Faith is not an airy glow, lacking substance; faith has content, and that content centres on Jesus.[15] While the New Testament gives no place to a caste of high-class scholars, whose "knowledge" puts them in a su-

14. Hans Dieter Betz, *Galatians* (Philadelphia, 1979), p. 116. George S. Duncan, commenting on this reference to knowledge, says, "we remember how often Paul reminds his readers of the truths on which their religious convictions are based; cf. 'we know' in Rom. viii.22, 28; 2 Cor. v.1" (*The Epistle of Paul to the Galatians* [London, 1939], p. 64).

15. Cf. Ronald A. Ward, "In all genuine faith there is an exercise of the mind in which statements are apprehended. For example, the preacher says that 'Christ died for our sins.' Some men do not know this. After they have heard the preacher they do know it. Then they put their trust in Christ and exercise 'saving faith.' They have not gone back on what the preacher said. They have embraced it at a deeper level, at which they have given themselves to the living Christ. In their very faith they had *knowledge*, knowledge of a truth and of him who is truth" (*Commentary on 1 & 2 Timothy & Titus* [Waco, 1974], p. 45).

perior position, it continually emphasizes the importance of Christian conviction. There is all the difference in the world between someone who can say, "I know", and someone who can say no more than, "it would seem possible to lay down the supposition that—". The objective fact of the saving work of Christ on the cross puts the knowledge of salvation on a different level from scholarly hypotheses.

KNOWLEDGE AND LOVE

There is an instructive paragraph at the beginning of 1 Corinthians 8, the passage where Paul begins his discussion of the problem posed to Christians of his day by the use of meat that had been offered to idols. "We know that we all have knowledge", he writes (v. 1). This may be a quotation from the letter the Corinthians had written to him (some translations take it this way, as NEB, NIV mg.). This is not unlikely, but we have no way of being sure. In any case Paul makes the words his own. There may be something of a rebuke to the Corinthians in the word "all"; the knowledge on which they prided themselves was no big deal, for all, even the humblest of Christians, have knowledge. It is characteristic of believers and not some great boon given to a chosen few. Paul immediately adds, "Knowledge puffs up but love builds up". He is not saying that knowledge is unimportant (the whole of his correspondence in which he conveys knowledge to Christians in a variety of needs and a variety of places makes it clear that he sees knowledge as very important for the servant of Christ). He is saying that love matters more than anything. A loveless knowledge is not Christian knowledge. Knowledge by itself may make a person proud, a fact attested only too often in the history of the human race. It is love that builds us up and makes us strong Christians.

Paul goes on to point out that our knowledge is at best partial: "If anyone thinks he knows something, he does not yet know as he must know" (v. 2). Interestingly, although he is cutting down to size some Corinthians who felt that they were very knowledgeable Christians, he does not belittle knowledge. He speaks of knowing "as he must know", where "must" is a strong word. Growth in knowledge is not an option for the Christian: it is a necessity.

Then his argument takes an unexpected twist. We expect something like, "If anyone loves God, this person has real knowledge". But this is not what Paul says. He says, "If anyone loves God, this person is known by him" (v. 3). It is not our knowledge of God that is the really significant thing but his knowledge of us. Of course, God knows everybody. But he knows his own in some special sense, and that sense is connected with love. Paul connects knowledge and love elsewhere. Thus he tells us that God demonstrates his love in the death of Christ for us (Rom. 5:8), where "demonstrates" means something like "shows us", "causes us to know". And at the culmination of his great chapter on love (1 Cor. 13) he says, "I shall know as I am known" (1 Cor. 13:12). The perfection of love does not play down the importance of knowledge. Rather, when love reaches its consummation, full and complete knowledge will have a place.[16]

It is not without its importance that John precedes one of his two statements that "God is love" with the words, "we have known and believed the love which God has within us" (1 John 4:16). For John, knowledge, love, and believing are all-important concepts, and it is interesting to see the three combined in this way. We may fairly infer that they belong together, so that the love and faith of which John writes do not exist apart from an element of knowledge. Paul also can pray that the love of the Philippians "may abound yet more and more in knowledge and all discernment" (Phil. 1:9). For both writers love is more than sentimentality and is linked with knowledge.

The knowledge of God is an integral part of the new covenant which means so much to the writer to the Hebrews. In his quota-

16. Cf. R. C. H. Lenski, "As God's direct and all-penetrating knowledge takes into account every one of his children already in eternity and, of course, through all of life, so we, too, shall at last know God directly and completely to the highest degree in which this is possible for his children" (*The Interpretation of St. Paul's First and Second Epistles to the Corinthians* [Minneapolis, 1963], p. 571).

tion from Jeremiah 31 he includes God's words, "they will all know me, from the least to the greatest of them" (Heb. 8:11). Now it is central to his argument that Christ has instituted the new covenant in his sacrifice of himself. This results in the decisive putting away of sin (Heb. 10:18), and, as we now learn, in the knowledge of God as well. We would not know God as we do were it not for Christ's atoning work.

Ignorance with all the limitations that it implies is part of this life, and as long as we are on earth we are going to be fettered by some of those limitations. But for Christians ignorance is not the last word. Paul regards knowledge, thoroughgoing knowledge, as characteristic of the life to come, when we enter fully into all that the salvation Christ has won for us means. And there is a foretaste of that here and now. Paul prays for his correspondents, "that Christ may dwell in your hearts through faith, so that, being rooted and founded in love, you may be strong to comprehend together with all the saints what is the breadth and length and depth and height and to know the love of Christ that passes knowledge . . ." (Eph. 3:17-19). And, of course, for Paul love is known because of what Christ has done in dying for us (Rom. 5:8).

The removal of ignorance and the gift of knowledge are not often specifically linked to the cross. But consider that ignorance and sin are closely related, as we saw earlier in this study salvation and knowledge are. Ignorance always leads people away from God (the lost are "them who know not God" with which is linked "them that disobey the gospel of our Lord Jesus" [2 Thess. 1:8]), whereas salvation may be understood in terms of the knowledge of the Father (1 John 2:14), a knowledge that is brought about only by the Son (Matt. 11:27) in a revelation that is seen nowhere as clearly as at the cross. It is knowledge of the Son (Phil. 3:10), or of both (John 17:3), a knowledge in which grace and truth are multiplied (2 Pet. 1:2). It is knowledge of the truth (2 John 1), of the mystery of the kingdom (Mark 4:11), of the mystery of Christ (Eph. 3:4), of the love of Christ (Eph. 3:19), which love is seen on the cross (Gal. 2:20); it is the knowledge of Christ and the power of his resurrection and the fellowship of his sufferings (Phil. 3:10). It is a knowledge that Christ has been raised from the dead (Rom. 6:9), and that he who raised the Lord Jesus will raise us with Jesus and present us along with him (2 Cor. 4:14). The knowledge of the Son of God is part of the process of arriving at the stature of the perfect man, the consummation of Christ's saving work (Eph. 4:13).

I do not see how it can be seriously disputed that part of our understanding of the atonement must be that the work of Christ liberates us from ignorance and brings us into a knowledge which may be described in various ways. It is knowing God, it is knowing Christ, it is knowing the truth, it is knowing the riches of God's glory, it is knowing the grace of our Lord Jesus Christ, and there are other ways of putting it. Express it how you will, it means that the worst aspects of human ignorance have been dispelled for those who have come into the knowledge that God has for his people. Salvation and knowledge are perhaps not as directly connected in the New Testament as are some other ways of looking at the cross. But ignorance leads people away from God, and salvation is understood as the knowledge of God, of Christ, of truth, none of which is attained by human endeavour. They are always seen as the gift of God, and salvation, however it is expressed, is always seen in the New Testament as the result of the cross. Thus it is important to include the dispelling of ignorance and the entrance of real knowledge as part of Christ's atonement.

This does not mean that Christianity is to be understood as a form of Gnosticism or as a game for the intellectual elite. It is not a knowledge of esoteric heavenly mysteries of which the New Testament speaks, nor is Christianity to be viewed as a puzzle, so hard to understand that only the intellectually gifted can cope with it. It is knowledge of a person that is meant (cf. 2 Tim. 1:12), and that knowledge is open to the humblest. As this knowledge is always a knowledge that is a gift of God, it is a gift that he may bestow on anyone, no matter how limited his or her capacity for other kinds of knowledge. And however it be described, salvation throughout the New Testament is always the gift of God. The knowledge God gives may then be fairly linked with other aspects of salvation as being due to Christ's saving work.

CHAPTER FIVE

The Answer to Loneliness

In the creation story we read, "It is not good for the man to be alone" (Gen. 2:18); the narrative goes on to tell us how woman was created. It is not good for a member of the race to be alone. Throughout history people have lived in groups, in tribes, in villages and cities. They have given their loyalties to regions and nations. They have recognized that they belong with other members of the race and that a solitary life is an impoverished life. It is true that from time to time solitary people have made their appearance, people like hermits, who have lived out their lives in isolation from other people. I am no authority on this sort of life, but it seems to me that not many of them have really enjoyed their existence or felt that they had achieved much. They felt that it was right to live in solitude so that they could give themselves to prayer and meditation, but I do not know that many of them (if any) claimed to live a full and abundant life. They certainly missed a good deal both in the way of enjoyment and of profit, for we learn from one another, we strengthen one another, and we bring joy to one another.

In modern times there have been some significant changes in the way we live. There has been a marked tendency for people to leave their hamlets and villages and to congregate in metropolises. In my own country, Australia, though there are enormous stretches of land on which people could live, in fact more than half the population lives in the capital cities of the various states (and, of course, many also live in cities other than capital cities or in large towns). This is not peculiar to one country or group of countries. It is not a trend that is found only in the developed nations, for example; it is to be seen in Third World countries as well as in those with more in the way of amenities. Big cities the world over tend to grow bigger, and the proportion of city-dwellers is on the increase in almost every land. Sometimes this is due to circumstances beyond the control of those who uproot themselves. Policies may be such that agriculture is no longer profitable; those on the land cannot make a living for themselves and their dependents and, looking at the city as it were through rose-colored spectacles, they see it as a place where goodies abound. Young people are attracted by the variety of amenities available in the city which cannot be found in the country. For good reasons and bad there is a marked drift to the cities.

But this brings a new factor into living because the big modern city is not a community. In a village everyone knows everyone else and everyone has a slot in village life into which he or she can slip more or less comfortably. But in our cities people tend to go their own ways and to neglect one another. Every now and then our newspapers or our television cameras bring us news of someone found living in startling isolation right in the middle of a huge conglomeration of citizens. And even among people who live a normal city life and have workmates and social acquaintances there is often a good deal of strain. There may be nobody in such a situation who can be called a close friend, nobody to whom one can confide intimate details of life and its problems. The result is a great deal of stress, which may issue in mental illness and, all too often, breakdown. Even for those who are not so maladjusted as to seek psychiatric help there is often a good deal of strain. The "stress factor" must be taken into consideration in many of our situations, and living together in our big cities has proved to be far from an unmixed blessing. Paradoxically it has led to a good deal of isolation. There would be few city-dwellers who have not at times felt very much alone. The tramping of the myriads of feet of complete strangers passing by does not reassure us. It simply emphasizes the sense of our aloneness.

A distressing feature of modern life is the large number of young people who have run away from home and are living on the streets. Sometimes they become members of a gang or other group, but all too often they are simply alone, with a loneliness that can be very wearing and which in too many cases leads to suicide. A per-· son who is quite alone is a very defenceless person. It is easy in such a situation to feel that God (if, of course, there is a God in the view of such people) does not care. One is simply godforsaken.

Another acute problem for the modern world is the suffering involved in many illnesses. People who have watched loved ones die in agony with some forms of cancer, for example, are apt to ask, "Why doesn't God stop this kind of suffering?" from which it is but a small step to, "Is there a God at all?" At such a time the world seems godforsaken. Then there are those who live their lives under some grave handicap, people crippled by a debilitating disease per-haps, or suffering from a severe mental illness. And what are we to say of those who suffer such birth defects that their whole life is impoverished? Questions like these are unanswerable given our present state of knowledge, but that does not mean that they are not going to be asked.

The problem does not concern our individual consciousness alone, though that is obviously very important to each of us. It con-cerns our whole world. There are terrible earthquakes in which people suffer and die for no fault of their own. There are cyclones and tornadoes and typhoons and other terrible storms that lead to loss of life, to the maiming of people who have not engaged in provocation of any sort. Disasters like floods or volcanic eruptions are no respecters of persons. The human race is not proof against its environment.

And what are we to say of the horrors we inflict on one another? There are human inventions like the torture chambers of secret police and concentration camps. As I write these words, there is a situation in Lebanon in which members of one of the strong militias of that country are besieging a camp of refugees and refusing to allow any food to be given to the starving even though it is widely known that the hungry have exhausted their food supplies and have been reduced to eating dogs, rats, and other food that would never feature on a menu from choice. "Why doesn't God do something?" people ask, "Where is God when such terrible evils take place?" To many modern people it has become quite impossible to believe in the existence of a good God when natural disasters can be so damaging and when the actions of evil people can inflict such hardship on the innocent. Someone has spoken of our generation as one whose creed is unreasoning optimism and which is knee-deep in blood. There is a good deal to support this understanding. Without any reason we keep hoping that everything will turn out all right in the end. And in the meantime we ruthlessly pursue our private ends, no matter what the cost to other people. What with official wars, undeclared wars, purges, gang executions, armed robberies, domestic murders, to name but a few of our ways of getting rid of one another, we have managed to slaughter our fellows on an unprecedented scale.

We rarely stop to think how this affects our understanding of God, except occasionally to ask why he doesn't stop it all. When Frances Young speaks of "our sense of the absence or callousness of God", this corresponds to something in the way most people regard our world. But this does not mean that we are right. As she also says, "The problem we have is Job's problem writ large; and Job's protests are our protests. We need the solution he was offered: a sense of the presence of God."[1]

FORSAKEN BY GOD

"A sense of the presence of God." This leads me to one of the most horrifying passages in all of Scripture, that in which Jesus, as he hung on the cross, cried out, "My God, my God, why did you forsake me?" (Matt. 27:46; Mark 15:34). On the face of it these words indicate that in the hour of his deepest need Jesus was forsaken by the Father in whom he had placed such trust. Pious and earnest Christians have always found these words very difficult,

1. Frances Young, *Can These Bones Live?* (London, 1982), p. 80.

and the exegesis of the passages containing them has taken some curious twists.

Some have found this "a hard saying", too hard, indeed, to accept. They have taken refuge in a distinction between what one feels and what is actually the case. T. R. Glover has given the classic statement of this position with his words, "I have sometimes thought there never was an utterance that reveals more amazingly the distance between feeling and fact."[2] This type of explanation has been widely popular, probably because it points to something real in the experience of every one of us. We all know what it is to feel desolate. Everyone is against us, we think, and God does not care. But then when the worst moments pass and we can think more clearly we realize that all this was a delusion, that God does care and that we must not take our feelings in our worst moments as giving an accurate account of the realities of the situation.

But are we justified in taking our misunderstandings of our troubles as being an accurate indication of Jesus' thinking at the moment of his death? There seems to be no reason for this. We cannot say that because we so easily are weak and mistaken, this is what happened to Jesus. We should not overlook the fact that even in this saying Jesus spoke of "my" God: his trust was still real and still strong. At the very moment of his forsakenness he could speak of God as his own God. And it is important that he does not rail on God or criticize him in any way. The words are words of perplexity, but they are also words of trust. Surely Jesus was looking clear-sightedly at what was happening, and to say that he has complete-

2. T. R. Glover, *The Jesus of History* (London, 1917), p. 192. There is often a reluctance to accept the words. Karl Barth, for example, can say, "In the end He was absolutely alone in the world, even to the point of asking (Mk. 15^{34}) whether God Himself, and God especially had not forsaken Him" (*Church Dogmatics*, IV, *The Doctrine of Reconciliation*, 2 [Edinburgh, 1958], p. 168). But Jesus did not ask "Whether?" but "Why?" God had forsaken him. Elsewhere, however, Barth can cite the cry of dereliction and say, "The Gospels do not conceal the fact, but state it, that His death is a problem of the first magnitude. . . . The darkness of His end is a true and final darkness" (*ibid.*, pp. 250f.).

ly misunderstood the situation is no explanation at all. It is much more likely that we have misunderstood him than that he has misunderstood God.[3]

It is perhaps important that there are different ways of crying out. There can be the cry of a crowd baying for blood (Acts 25:24) or the cry of evil spirits (Acts 8:7). But there can also be the cry of one who calls on God, knowing that his own power is unavailing in the distress in which he finds himself. And, as E. Stauffer reminds us, there can be "a crying after God himself" (as distinct from a cry for help). Of Jesus' prayer he says, "It is a cry in which the shattering and impotence of his whole being are manifested."[4] When we feel that God has forsaken us, it matters very much whether we cry out in a spirit of complaint and peevishness or whether we cry after God,[5] with a full realization of our utter impotence and a concern for his glory.

3. R. W. Dale says it well: "I shrink from saying that even in my calmest and brightest hours I have a knowledge of God and the ways of God which is truer than Christ had, even in His agony. I dare not stand before His cross and tell Him that even for a moment He imagines something concerning God which is not a fact and cannot be a fact. I prefer to believe that it was necessary for the great ends of human redemption that when Christ was on the cross He should submit to the awful suffering arising from 'the loss of the sense of God's presence'" (*The Atonement* [London, 1902], p. xli).

4. TDNT, I, p. 627. He further says, "this *boan* does not ring out unheard in cold and empty space. The man who relies on himself and on his own power is silenced in his distress. The man who knows that he confronts a divine Thou presses on to God in his distress and brings all his need before Him. The man who does not know this kind of prayer is overwhelmed by loneliness. Biblical man knows a profounder solitariness, namely, the abyss of isolation from God"; he cites, "Out of the depths I cry to you, O LORD" (Ps. 130:1).

5. L. Goppelt says that Jesus' cry in Mark 15:34 "seeks God out of dereliction" (TDNT, VI, p. 153, n. 41). Frances Young speaks of "the presence of God in the midst of all that denies him", and she says, "It is the reality of atonement—at-one-ment being the integration of the deep tensions built into God's world, an integration effected through the reality of God's presence" (*Can These Bones Live?* pp. 60f., 63; the thought is repeated on

These days it is common to have scholars taking notice of the fact that the words Jesus used are the opening words of Psalm 22, a Psalm that begins with the note of tragedy and ends on that of trust. Now despite the strength of the words we are considering, we need not think that Jesus had lost faith in the Father. As we have just seen, Jesus still recognized the Father as his God and cried out to him. There is certainly trust here.

But it is another thing to say that the words are no more than a shorthand way of indicating that Jesus was consoling himself in his suffering by reciting a comforting psalm. The view is put this way by D. E. Nineham: "Taken as a whole, this Psalm is anything but a cry of despair; it is the prayer of a righteous sufferer who yet trusts fully in the love and protection of God and is confident of being vindicated by him. . . . There is some evidence that among the ancient Jews the opening words of this Psalm were interpreted in the light of the rest of it and recognized as an effective form of prayer for help in time of trouble." He thinks that Mark may have seen Jesus as "making his own the Psalmist's expression of complete faith and confidence in God".[6] Such views are widely held, and they are much more comforting than understanding the cry of dereliction to mean that Jesus was really forsaken by the Father.

But such positions scarcely do justice to the words used. In the first instance we cannot be sure that Jesus was in fact quoting the Psalm. William Blight reminds us that people who have studied the

---

p. 81). These are helpful thoughts, though it may be questioned whether the presence of God itself effects atonement. It is the action of God rather than his presence that brings about atonement.

6. D. E. Nineham, *The Gospel of St Mark* (Harmondsworth, 1963), p. 428. Nineham puts this view alongside that which takes the words "more or less at their face value" without giving a final verdict between them. Incidentally, the only reason he cites for seeing this as an ancient Jewish prayer for help is a late midrash cited by Dalman, and he does not notice that Dalman goes on to say, "one realises how foreign such a Judaism must have been to our Lord" (Gustaf Dalman, *Jesus-Jeshua* [London, 1929], p. 207; Dalman himself favors the view that the words "exhibited the state of mind of one who even in the travail of death was conscious that he belonged to God . . .").

Scriptures long and closely and who esteem them highly are apt to express their thoughts in biblical language. He thinks that this was true of Jesus in the present instance: "When on the Cross He felt acutely His isolation from God and man. 'Cursed is every one that hangeth on a cross' was a statement with which He had long been familiar. He felt alone, deserted: and He said so: in Scriptural words. But He was not quoting at all."[7] It is, of course, impossible to prove that Blight is correct. But it is equally impossible to prove that Jesus was in fact quoting. Both possibilities must be kept in mind.

But in the second instance, even if he was quoting from the Psalm we cannot assume that his use of the opening words implies that he was reciting the whole. Nor can we say that because he used the opening words he meant them to include everything that followed. It is true that there are some comforting words later in the Psalm, but if Jesus meant them it is fair to ask why he did not use them. Scarcely any words in the whole Psalm are as far from expressing trust and consolation as these words. The objection lodged long ago by Maynard Smith still stands: "the awful cry which startled the onlookers cannot be reconciled with a devotional exercise."[8]

We must bear in mind that these are the only words Matthew and Mark record as having been spoken from the cross. Luke and John record other sayings, but our first two Evangelists record this saying only and do not qualify it. This gives the words special emphasis, and as they stand they point to a lonely and horrible death. If the Evangelists really meant that Jesus was expressing his confidence rather than a sense of being forsaken, it would have taken no more than an additional phrase to make this clear. They could have said that Jesus was reciting the whole Psalm, for example. Their leaving these words and these words alone to stand in stark simplicity must be significant. They are recording dereliction, a real abandonment by God.

7. ET, LXVIII (1956-57), p. 285.
8. H. Maynard Smith, *Atonement* (London, 1925), p. 155.

This does not mean that Jesus ceased to trust the Father. The very cry "My God" with its possessive pronoun "My" relates the speaker to the God who has forsaken him. He has a strong and robust faith in the one who calls on God even though he knows that God has forsaken him. Kosuke Koyama cites Luther, "He flees to God against God! O strong faith!" and goes on to speak of Jesus, along with Jeremiah, as putting trust "in the forsaking God! Theirs is no longer the faith built upon God's obvious answer. They believed in God even though God did not answer!"⁹ I do not think that Koyama has penetrated into the depths of this cry, as his linking of Jesus with Jeremiah shows. Jesus was really forsaken whereas Jeremiah only felt himself to be forsaken. But there is value in his recognition of Jesus' trust in the Father in his most difficult hour. Trust in God "even though God did not answer" is the profoundest trust of all, and we surely see it here.

A REAL ABANDONMENT

Some recent writers are taking seriously the concept of dereliction. Thus Jürgen Moltmann reasons this way: "The unparalleled claim of Jesus includes the forgiveness of sins here on earth, through the exercise of the divine right of grace. By identifying himself with God in this way, Jesus was clearly assuming that God identified himself with him and his words. But anyone who lived and preached so close to God, his kingdom and his grace, and associated the decision of faith with his own person, could not regard his being handed over to death on the cross as one accursed as a mere mishap, a human misunderstanding or a final trial, but was bound to experience it as rejection by the very God whom he had dared to call 'My Father'. When we look at his non-miraculous and helpless suffering and dying in the context of his preaching and his life, we understand how his misery cried out to heaven: it is the experience of abandonment by God in the knowledge that God is not

9. Kosuke Koyama, *No Handle on the Cross* (London, 1976), p. 75. The passage of Jeremiah on which he relies is Jer. 20:7-9, 14, 18.

distant but close; does not judge but shows grace. And this, in full consciousness that God is close at hand in his grace, to be abandoned and delivered up to death as one rejected, is the torment of hell."[10] Similarly Pannenberg can say, "Jesus died this death of the sinner because his death on the cross sealed his exclusion from God's nearness."[11] Both are pointing to a death of unimaginable horror.

Moltmann points to the deaths of other people, sometimes deaths by crucifixion, and goes on, "None of this distinguishes the death of Jesus from other crosses in the history of human suffering. Not until we understand his abandonment by the God and Father whose imminence and closeness he had proclaimed in a unique, gracious and festive way, can we understand what was distinctive about his death. Just as there was a unique fellowship with God in his life and preaching, so in his death there was a unique abandonment by God."[12] Clearly Moltmann regards Jesus' abandonment by God as something to be taken seriously. It is to be accepted, not explained away, and accepted moreover as the really significant thing about the death of the Saviour. Some such position must surely be accepted if we are to place any credence at all on the teaching of the New Testament. We may not like it, but the cry of dereliction is well attested and there is something hollow about the attempts that have been made to evade the force of its teaching. It must be seen as authentic and as teaching us something important about Christ's saving activity.[13]

10. Jürgen Moltmann, *The Crucified God* (London, 1974), pp. 147f.

11. Wolfhart Pannenberg, *Jesus—God and Man* (Philadelphia, 1968), p. 270.

12. *The Crucified God*, p. 149. He further asks, "Why did Jesus die?" and answers, "He died not only because of the understanding of the law by his contemporaries or because of Roman power politics, but ultimately because of his God and Father. The torment in his torments was this abandonment by God" (*ibid.*).

13. Cf. William L. Lane, "The cry has a ruthless authenticity which provides the assurance that the price of sin has been paid in full" (*The Gospel according to Mark* [Grand Rapids, 1974], p. 573).

We should understand this cry also as something like the consummation of Christ's becoming man. When he came to this earth, Jesus did not do so in triumph and majesty but in lowliness and rejection. He was born into a peasant family and he lived his life in a backwater. His teaching was for the most part given in towns and villages in obscure Galilee with only occasional visits to Jerusalem, which, in any case, was not one of the world's great cities. Throughout his entire life he took a lowly place and in the end he died the death of a criminal. Walther Künneth has written a book about the significance of the resurrection of Christ in which among other things he points to the humiliation involved in the incarnation with its nadir at the cross: "The humiliation of the Son of God reaches its decisive depth on the cross, in keeping with the utter reprobation of mankind and the loneliness of separation from God in the judgment of death as the fruit of humanity's sin."[14] There can be no doubt that loneliness, a sense of isolation from God, is one of the most painful experiences of this human life. Had Christ not undergone it his human life would have lacked one dimension all too characteristic of our way of life.

To be really one with us Christ had to know something of our loneliness. But he did more. He bore the loneliness attendant, not on his own sin for he had none, but on ours. He endured the godforsakenness that was our due. He entered our loneliness to take it away, and because of what he has done we know the fulfilment of the Old Testament promise "I will never leave you nor forsake you" (Heb. 13:5; cf. Deut. 31:6, 8).

Perhaps we should understand the dereliction as a manifestation of the wrath of God against all evil,[15] a wrath that Christ endured in his saving death. Alan Richardson cites Mark 15:34 as one

14. Walther Künneth, *The Theology of the Resurrection* (London, 1965), p. 124.

15. John R. W. Stott can say, "My own wish, I confess, is that Professor Moltmann had emphasized more strongly that it was with the *spiritually* outcast, not just the *socially* outcast, that is to say, with sinners not just criminals, that Jesus identified on the cross" (*The Cross of Christ* [Leicester, 1986], pp. 216f.).

of the passages that justify him in saying, "The cross of Christ is the visible, historical revelation of the *orgē tou Theou*: it is the supreme revelation of the wrath of God against all ungodliness and unrighteousness of men" (his other passages are Rom. 1:18; 2 Cor. 5:21).[16] C. C. Ryrie interprets the saying as comprehensive; he comments on it in these terms: "All that is involved is inscrutable, but He gave Himself, He was made sin, He bore our sins, and His soul was an offering for sin. His work was to bear sin."[17] However we understand it, we must take the passage to point to a real, if undefined separation between the Father and the Son.[18] Anything less fails to do justice to the words.

GETHSEMANE

We must bear in mind that the cry of dereliction does not stand alone. The two Evangelists who record it record also that Jesus was in a veritable agony in the Garden of Gethsemane as he contemplated the death he would die. Matthew says that as Jesus went to pray he "began to be distressed and troubled" (Matt. 26:37), and Mark that he "began to be amazed and troubled" (Mark 14:33).[19]

16. Alan Richardson, *An Introduction to the Theology of the New Testament* (London, 1958), p. 77. Cf. Donald Guthrie, "the consciousness of Jesus that his mission would end in death and would involve an act of substitution would be a sufficient explanation of the sense of separation" (*New Testament Theology* [Leicester, 1981], p. 446).

17. Charles Caldwell Ryrie, *Biblical Theology of the New Testament* (Chicago, 1982), p. 69.

18. "Jesus saw himself cut off from the relationship to God that was for him life itself" (Leonhard Goppelt, *Theology of the New Testament,* I [Grand Rapids, 1981], p. 189); "He saw himself abandoned by God, condemned" (*ibid.*, p. 227).

19. Matthew has *lypeisthei kai adēmonein* while Mark has *ekthambeisthai* in place of the first verb. G. Bertram comments that the theological significance of Mark's expression "has always been found in its antidocetic character" (TDNT, III, p. 7). It points to Jesus' real manhood. Vincent Taylor finds these words "one of the most important statements in Mk.", and he notes Lohmeyer's comment, "The Gk words depict the utmost degree of un-

There can be no doubt that these Evangelists are describing Jesus' horror at the death he was about to die.[20] Now death is not an attractive prospect for those of the human race, but it is not usual for people to face it with the horror so plain in Gethsemane. We cannot feel that it was the death that is the common lot of humanity that caused Jesus' distress. It was rather the fact that he faced a death far different from that which others face, a death that included abandonment by the Father. Ronald Wallace reminds us of the words of John Owen, that this took place "when there was no hand or instrument outwardly appearing to put him to any suffering or cruciating torment", and proceeds, "It is as if he were suffering now solely from the hand of God himself—or at least in a region and manner quite beyond our understanding."[21] We should be clear that what happened in Gethsemane was not the normal run of human happenings: it pointed to a horror of which the rest of the human race knows nothing.

Jesus' prayer in the Garden was, "My Father, if it is possible, let this cup pass from me" (Matt. 26:39; cf. Mark 14:36), where the "cup" may be the cup of wrath or the cup of suffering, both of which are found in the Old Testament (Isa. 51:17; Ezek. 23:32-

---

bounded horror and suffering", and Rawlinson's verdict that *adēmonein* is "suggestive of shuddering awe" (*The Gospel according to St. Mark* [London, 1959], p. 552). J. B. Lightfoot says that this verb "describes the confused, restless, half-distracted state, which is produced by physical derangement, or by mental distress, as grief, shame, disappointment, etc." (*Saint Paul's Epistle to the Philippians* [London, 1908], p. 123).

20. Karl Barth brings out something of the horror: "We are told of an *ekthambeisthai* of Jesus (Mk. 14[33]); of a horror which gripped Him in face of the frightful event which confronted Him; of an *adēmonein;* of a foreboding from which there was no escape, in which He could find no help or comfort, which was only foreboding; of an *agōnia* (Lk. 22[44]) in which His sweat fell to the earth like drops of blood; of a *lypeisthei,* a sorrow, a heaviness, an oppression which was 'even unto death' (Mt. 26[38])" (*The Doctrine of Reconciliation,* I, p. 265).

21. Ronald S. Wallace, *The Atoning Death of Christ* (London, 1981), p. 100.

33).[22] G. Stählin points out that the former would mean that "by taking it Jesus fears a disruption of the loving fellowship in which His existence rests. And the sign that he must still drink it is the cry of dereliction on the cross."[23] This interpretation cannot be said to be beyond any possible doubt, but it does seem the probable under-standing of the words. Jesus' perturbation in the Garden, then, is due to the kind of death he faced.

Many have faced death calmly. Socrates is often selected as an example of the way a wise man faces the end of this earthly life. Clearly he was quite cheerful as he drank the hemlock. He asked for a cock to be sacrificed to Asclepius, which may be understood as pointing to some kind of victory, for it was usual to do this on recovery from sickness. The calm conversation with friends is a far cry from the agony of Christ in Gethsemane. But then, the gentle death that Socrates died was a long way from the atoning death of Jesus. Socrates passed from this life, but he never encountered the full horror of death. Jesus did, and that was what was distinctive about Calvary.

Christian martyrs such as those executed in the early persecu-tions also faced death calmly or even sometimes ecstatically. Death held no terrors for them, and their faith in Christ saw them through all that death meant. But Jesus himself did not experience such a death. It was not that he lacked courage, for the story of his life shows him acting with considerable bravery on more than one oc-casion. It is impossible to hold that he faced with dread an ex-perience that many of his followers took with exultation. It was not death as such that caused this depth of feeling, but the kind of death Jesus faced.

Paul tells us that "Christ redeemed us from the law's curse, having become a curse for us, because it is written, 'Cursed is everyone who hangs on a tree'" (Gal. 3:13), where clearly the

22. G. E. Ladd has no doubts. He says, "the awfulness of the cup of God's wrath against sin is so bitter that he cannot but cry out for deliverance—'if it were possible' (Mk. 15:34)" (*A Theology of the New Tes-tament* [Grand Rapids, 1975], p. 191).

23. TDNT, V, p. 437, n. 386.

curse of God is in some way connected with the death Jesus died. Paul puts it another way when he says, "him who knew no sin he [i.e., God] made sin for us in order that we might become God's righteousness in him" (2 Cor. 5:21). Both these passages link Jesus' death with evil and bring out the fact that an atoning death is very different from the other deaths people die. We are reminded of the words of Habakkuk's prayer, "Your eyes are too pure to look on evil" (Hab. 1:13).[24] It seems that what Matthew and Mark are saying when they record the cry of dereliction is that in his death Jesus was so closely identified with sin and the sinners for whose salvation he was dying that the close communion that had hitherto linked him with the Father was broken. That would account for the various unusual things that are related about the way Jesus died. I am not aware of anything else that does.

It may be that this is the way we should understand the passage in Hebrews that tells us that Jesus suffered "outside the gate" (Heb. 13:12). The writer is using the symbolism of the Day of Atonement ceremonies according to which the carcass of the sin offering was burned outside the camp. This is more or less equivalent to the idea of dereliction expressed liturgically.[25]

24. Charles L. Taylor comments on the question to which this leads up: "the question fundamentally concerns not so much the world as God himself. Why is God this kind of a God? Here is one of the most important steps in the history of Jewish speculation" (IB, VI, p. 985). D. Martyn Lloyd-Jones links this passage with the cry of dereliction and says, "if He was to be made sin, and sin was to be punished in His body, it meant that He must be separated from the Father. . . . He took the problem He did not understand to God and left it there. We may say with reverence that the Lord Jesus, though perhaps not fully understanding because He had been made man, nevertheless went on, confident that God's will is always right, and that a holy God will never command anything that is wrong" (*From Fear to Faith* [London, 1961], pp. 28-29).

25. P. E. Hughes points to the "unholy ground" outside the gate of the city on which Jesus made his sacrifice of himself and comments, "How extraordinary, indeed shocking, to the Hebrew mind, to be told that he did this *in order to sanctify the people through his own blood,* precisely on this unsanctified territory! The very concept must have seemed self-contradictory"

We should also reflect on the significance of passages like that in which Jesus says, "the Son of man is delivered up into the hands of men and they will kill him" (Mark 9:31; cf. 10:33; 14:41; Matt. 17:22; 26:2, 45; Luke 9:44;[26] 18:32; 24:7). Jesus does not say that the men in question will take the initiative. They will kill him, indeed, but before that another will deliver him up for this death. This other cannot be anyone except God, and passages of this kind bear witness to the truth that God was active in bringing about the death of his Son;[27] it was God who sacrificed him. This is given some emphasis by Paul, who tells us that God "did not spare his own Son, but delivered him up for us all" (Rom. 8:32). The fact that the handing over of Jesus to death is the act of the Father receives emphasis.[28] D. Martyn Lloyd-Jones can say, "God acted through men, through the instrumentality of men, but the action

---

(A Commentary on the Epistle to the Hebrews [Grand Rapids, 1979], p. 579). A. Nairne views "that criminal execution" as "like—not an ancient sacrifice, but the offscouring of a sacrifice" (The Epistle of Priesthood [Edinburgh, 1913], p. 423). Such comments as these bring out the "unholiness" of Jesus' sacrifice of himself and thus the separation from God implied as Hebrews sees it.

26. I. H. Marshall says of the verb "will be delivered up" here that "it is used in the passive of the action of God" (The Gospel of Luke [Exeter and Grand Rapids, 1978], p. 394).

27. Cf. Lane, "More than simply the coming of an individual into another's power, the term connotes the actual fulfilment of God's will as expressed in Scripture" (The Gospel according to Mark, p. 337). Nineham remarks that "the Greek word paradidōmi . . . seems always in Mark to imply that the hand of God was in a special sense behind what was done" (The Gospel of St Mark, pp. 67n.). On the present passage he says, "we should probably find here the further idea that the whole Passion of Jesus had its ultimate ground in God's initiative and his concern for the salvation of men" (ibid., p. 249).

28. R. C. H. Lenski finds the idea of substitution here, for "only by being delivered up 'in our stead' could the Son have been delivered up 'in our behalf.' Remove substitution, and nothing of saving value in 'in our behalf' is left" (The Interpretation of St. Paul's Epistle to the Romans [Minneapolis, 1961], p. 567).

was the action of God!"[29] and he devotes several pages to emphasize the point. In these he draws attention to the agony in Gethsemane and the cry of dereliction. It is one thing to put up with a
death engineered by the forces of evil in defiance of the will of God
and quite another to undergo a death to which God has handed one
over. This is not a full statement of dereliction but it is not far short
of it.

THE BEARING OF SIN

There is a strand of New Testament teaching in which Jesus is
clearly seen as in some way separated from the Father in the death
he died. This strand of teaching is not congenial to our day and,
with such exceptions as Moltmann, receives little emphasis or even
attention in most modern writing. But it is there, and it should not
be overlooked, for, as I noticed earlier in this chapter, godforsakenness is part of the experience of this generation. Does the New Testament have anything to say to those who feel that God has left
them? It does. It tells us that the God who is the God of him who
was forsaken on the cross, indeed the God who delivered up his
Son to be forsaken on the cross, is the God of all the forsaken. It
tells us that in one aspect of his saving act Christ entered into all
that it means to be forsaken of God.[30] He has endured the worst that
sin can do and borne the separation from God that is the inevitable
consequence of sin. In this way he took our sin upon himself and
thus dealt with it decisively and permanently.

We should bear in mind the whole manner of Jesus' earthly
life. The lowliness of the incarnate Christ is not an accident. Why
did he not come as a ruler? Or a warrior? Or an ecclesiastic? Or a
sage? Why was he not someone who could be admired and looked
up to? His life was one of a lowliness incomprehensible to most of

29. *Romans 8:17-39* (Grand Rapids, 1980), pp. 303f.
30. Cf. H. Anderson, "in his death Christ has penetrated into the abyss of
all men's lostness" (*The Gospel of Mark* [London and Grand Rapids, 1981],
p. 346).

us. "The foxes have holes and the birds of heaven have roosting-places, but the Son of man has not where he may lay his head" (Luke 9:58). He depended on pious ladies for sustenance during his ministry (Luke 8:3). Clearly he lacked what we would call even the necessities of life. We might say that he lived a "godforsaken" life, at least as far as the amenities of this world go. And paradoxically it is in this life that God is revealed. We are not to forget that it was this godforsaken one who was raised. The resurrection is the proof that godforsakenness is not the whole story and is not to be understood in isolation. While it is true that the Father may abandon the Son to death, it is also true that the Father raises the Son from death. We are to see that God was in the crucifixion and God was in the resurrection even if we discern his power and his activity in different ways. The cross is eloquent testimony of God's deep concern for his people as he enters into their worst suffering, the suffering involved in dying alone. We must not forget that God was active in the cross. God "did not spare his own Son but delivered him up for us all" (Rom. 8:32); God "made him who knew no sin sin for us" (2 Cor. 5:21); God "so loved the world that he gave his only Son" (John 3:16). We misunderstand the cross unless we see that God was in it, and we misunderstand Christ's godforsakenness unless we see that God was somehow in that, too.[31] God was in the cross, but the cross is not alone. The cross leads on to the empty tomb, and neither is to be understood without the other.

We cannot understand the godforsakenness without considering the nature of the God who forsook his Son. The New Testament assures us that God is love (1 John 4:8, 16), which means more than that he occasionally experiences a tendency to act in a loving way. It means that love is his essential being. Whatever he does he does in love. For us being alone, being abandoned, is a tragic part

31. Moltmann asks, "How can God himself be in one who has been forsaken by God?" and answers this and other questions with a further question, "must one not understand this 'God and Father of Jesus Christ' completely in the light of what happened on the cross?" (*The Crucified God*, p. 190).

of life. We have all felt it at times, and for many in our day it is a tremendous problem. In the West at any rate we have lost the wider sense of the extended family, and even the nuclear family does not always offer a fulfilling and satisfying relationship. Many are grateful for the warmth of friends and sometimes for satisfying professional and shop floor relationships. But for far too many of us these are merely formal and external relationships; there is no sense of "Grapple them to thy soul with hoops of steel". Such relationships do not make us feel that we belong. Indeed, they may be characterized by criticisms and snide remarks from those who, rightly or wrongly, fancy that their achievements are superior and who drive us further into isolation. We so easily feel that nobody quite understands our singular situation and our peculiar difficulties. We can feel that we are quite on our own in a hostile world. This can become too hard to bear. The increase of suicides in our age, especially among the young, is understandable.

But the answer to our aloneness is another part of the meaning of the cross. In Ephesians 2 there is a strong statement about the way Christ has broken down the barriers that keep people apart. In the ancient world the division between Jew and Gentile was especially formidable, but "now in Christ Jesus you who formerly were far off have been brought near by the blood of Christ" (v. 13). Christ "is our peace" (v. 14), and by his death he has broken down the barriers between people who were most estranged from one another and also that between people and God. The result is that "through him we both have the introduction in one Spirit to the Father" (v. 18). "The peace of God", which is one of the great concepts of the New Testament, is a peace brought about by God's atoning work in Christ. The result is harmony, a harmony within the forgiven sinner who knows that his sin will no longer be held against him, a harmony between sinner and sinner because there is a bond that unites all who have had their sins put away in Christ, and above all a harmony between the forgiven and the God who forgave them.

With that we should place the last words of Jesus recorded in the First Gospel: "I am with you all the days until the close of the age" (Matt. 28:20). The certainty of the divine presence no matter what the circumstances has sustained believers through the world and through the centuries. The believer can never be completely alone. Fellowship with other believers in the church of God is a wonderful gift. But the most wonderful of all gifts we may cite in the words of the apostle Paul, who because of what Christ has done for us in his death can write, "I am persuaded that neither death nor life nor angels nor authorities nor things present nor things to come nor powers nor height nor depth nor any other created thing can separate us from the love of God which is in Christ Jesus our Lord" (Rom. 8:38-39).

CHAPTER SIX

The Answer to Sickness and Death

One of our great preoccupations in the modern world is with suffering. In earlier ages people probably suffered more, for they lacked modern painkillers and the medical skills that have cured many painful complaints. But they seem to have been more ready than we are to accept suffering as an inevitable part of life. We are greatly concerned about pain, physical or mental, and writing about it provides a good living for authors who like to harrow our feelings with their vivid descriptions of sufferings potential or actual, as in horror thrillers. Health concerns us deeply, and there are all kinds of fitness freaks, food faddists, and the like on the one hand and kindly healers on the other whose efforts are directed towards setting right the disorders arising from the inadequate functioning of our bodies for one reason or another. We go to great lengths to avoid suffering, and our advertisers go to even greater lengths to make sure we know that their products will remove our pain.

When people in the more developed countries contemplate those in the less developed countries, one of the foremost problems they encounter is that those countries lack proper medical care and as a result their inhabitants necessarily suffer a good deal of pain that could and should be prevented. Many of them die needlessly, for their diseases are curable, even preventable. One of the first things Christian missions do is to send medical personnel into the areas they seek to evangelize. I am, of course, objecting to none of this. I dislike pain as much as anybody and hold firmly that it is right and proper that we should try to avoid pain and sickness and that we should make the fullest possible attempts to send what medical help we can to those who lack it.

We are particularly concerned about death. We know that death is the normal end to earthly life: there is nothing unusual about it and we must all expect that it will befall us in due course. But death has become one of the taboos of our modern society. We have a very curious attitude to death. We do not face it; we do not think about it; we do not even speak about it unless we must. And when we must, we tend to use the language of rest instead of that of death (cf. "chapel of rest" for the funeral chapel and "garden of repose" for the cemetery). We live as though we do not have to die. Michael Green cites Arthur Koestler's words about some Americans who refuse to face the reality of death when "morticians endeavour to transform the dead, with lipstick and rouge, into horizontal members of a perennial cocktail party".[1] The equivalent, of course, is to be found in many nations. We know that we will face death at the end of this life of ours, but we steadfastly refuse to prepare for it.

It is interesting that we speak slightingly about the mid-Victorian attitude to life and in particular that we regard those ancestors of ours as prudes in sexual matters. As a generation we pride ourselves on our frankness about sex and congratulate ourselves on our deliverance from the hypocrisy and the ignorance that we think characterized our predecessors. More than one thing might be said about this, but the one point I want to make about it is that those mid-Victorians were much more frank and open about death than we are. They did not regard it as a taboo, a nameless horror that must be dismissed from their presence; they spoke about it freely. Few of them would have reached adult life without having stood beside more than one deathbed, whereas this would be an exceptional modern experience.

They did not think it strange to talk about being prepared for

1. Michael Green, *The Empty Cross of Jesus* (London and Downers Grove, 1984), p. 198.

death, whereas if someone were to introduce such a topic into one of our social gatherings we would be horrified and would change the subject promptly. We have become so afraid of death and all that it means that we have dismissed it from our presence. We consider it morbid to talk about it. We decline to prepare for it (other than in making our wills, and some of us even refuse to do even this). "Prepare to meet thy God" is an injunction our generation refuses to take seriously. If the words are used, they are probably on the lips of some comedian who is trying to raise a laugh with something that looks serious but which he knows his audience will take frivolously. Most people are not atheists and therefore they know that one day they will have to stand before God, but they stoutly refuse to make any preparation for what is surely the most critical moment they will ever face. All in all we have a very curious attitude toward death, and one that is far from healthy.

To all this we should add the drug scene. It is an indictment of our "enlightened" society that with all our knowledge and all our wealth it is the people of the "advanced" countries who are most given to drug addiction. Such addiction is not, of course, confined to them, but it is a more serious problem there than in other cultures. It is tragic that it is particularly a problem for our youth. People with all sorts of wonderful and exciting possibilities before them destroy themselves with heroin and other drugs, and so far no one has been able to work out a way of preventing this from happening. And this, of course, is no more than the most glaring example of a phenomenon that seems always to have been characteristic of the human race. It is only recently that we have become aware of the perils attending the use of tobacco and have made any attempt to cope with them. And there is very little public concern about alcohol, the most dangerous of them all as well as the oldest in common use. Through the centuries the physical and mental deterioration of addicts has been known, as also the temporary loss of faculties of those whose indulgence is not so constant. But it is still highly respectable to use this drug of dependence, and in many circles those who refuse it are regarded as very strange creatures, barely human.

THE BIBLE AND THE BODY

I am saying, then, that there is a good deal in the area of health that gives us concern in our modern society, and a good deal more that ought to give us concern. This is an area of life that must not be taken lightly, and especially by Christians, for the Bible puts a good deal of emphasis on the body. The body is a temple of the Holy Spirit (1 Cor. 6:19), and for Christians nothing could be more sacred than that. Believers are to be holy both in body and in spirit (1 Cor. 7:34). It thus comes as no surprise that the body is not meant for fornication (1 Cor. 6:13), and further that anyone who commits fornication sins against his own body (1 Cor. 6:18). Far from this, we are to present our bodies to God as a sacrifice, living, holy, and acceptable to him (Rom. 12:1), and again to present the members of our bodies to God as "implements of righteousness" (Rom. 6:13). Our bodies are "members of Christ" (1 Cor. 6:15). We are to glorify God with our bodies (1 Cor. 6:20). Christianity puts an emphasis on the body such as perhaps no other religion does. The body is important, and the Christian must give a good deal of thought to the way it is treated.[2]

There have been religions that took the body lightly. The Greeks, for example, could regard the soul as imprisoned within the body and evolve the jingle *sōma sēma,* "the body, a tomb". Even within Christianity there have been ascetics who thought they acquired merit before God by ill-treating the body. It is true that Paul speaks of putting to death the deeds of the body (Rom. 8:13) and further that he says, "I buffet my body and keep it in subjection" (1 Cor. 9:27), but he is referring to the disciplining of the body, not to deliberate ill-treatment of it with a view to gaining merit in God's sight. It is no part of the Christian way to let the bodily passions run riot, but we must bear in mind the difference between self-discipline (which is required of all Christians) and

2. Cf. E. Schweizer, "the flesh is not a sphere which is to be differentiated from other earthly things and which is intrinsically bad or especially dangerous. It becomes bad only when man builds his life on it" (TDNT, VII, p. 135).

self-torture (which is a perversion). Since the body matters, we must treat it properly. We notice a failure to value the body rightly in a different way in the attitudes that permeate our society. For example, when someone does wrong we may excuse him by saying, "His heart's in the right place". As long as his inner dispositions are correct, we imply, it matters little what he does with the body. But Christians can never take up that attitude. The body is part of God's good creation, and what we do in and with our bodies matters.

SALVATION AND THE BODY

Christ's salvation is concerned with the body as well as with the soul. Here we might notice an interesting piece of linguistics. When modern Christians use the verb "to save" and speak of people being saved they almost invariably refer to a spiritual process, whereas in the Gospels the verb is often applied to cures of the body. For example, the lady with the hemorrhage said to herself, "If only I touch his clothing I will be saved" (Matt. 9:21), and Jesus said to her, "Daughter, be cheerful, your faith has saved you" (Matt. 9:22). Matthew adds, "and the woman was saved from that hour". It may be fair to argue that the faith that is shown over and over in the cures is surely a faith that goes beyond the simple conviction that Jesus was a good healer, that it points beyond the cures to a genuine trust in Jesus, but even if this be accepted it is still true that "salvation" can be used to describe something that happened to the body. And we should not forget that Paul speaks of "the redemption of our body" (Rom. 8:23).

Jesus uses the exact expression, "your faith has saved you", of the sinful woman who wept over his feet and anointed them in the house of a Pharisee (Luke 7:50). On this occasion there is no thought of a physical act of healing, so we must understand the expression to mean salvation in a spiritual sense. We may perhaps reflect that of all the occasions on which the verb "save" is used of the cures Jesus effected not once does it refer to a single member of the body: it is always "your faith has saved you", never "your faith has saved your hand" or "your back" or any other part of the body. W. Foerster speaks of "the important phrase 'thy faith hath saved thee'" and goes on, "The choice of the word leaves room for the view that the healing power of Jesus and the saving power of faith go beyond physical life."[3] Now there cannot be the slightest doubt that salvation from sins (Matt. 1:21) is effected by the death of Jesus, so the possibility is raised that in an ultimate sense we are to understand the healing of the body as something that is embraced in the whole salvation that was brought about by Christ's sacrifice of himself. We may perhaps see this in Jesus' healing of the lame man lowered down through the roof before him. He first said to the man, "Child, your sins are forgiven", then a little later, "Rise, take up your pallet, and go to your home" (Mark 2:5, 11). If we cannot say that the man's sin was the cause of his lameness, we can say that at least in his salvation the two were closely linked.

Paul Tillich complains that too many of us have forgotten that "'Savior' means 'healer,' he who makes whole and sane what is broken and insane, in body and mind"; he further says, "saving the person is healing him."[4] Many modern thinkers insist that we can no longer think of healing a body but rather of healing a person: we treat the patient rather than the disease, for the physical and the spiritual are closely bound up together. This means that the process of salvation is to be understood as including the healing of the body: we cannot confine it to the purely spiritual. Dr Elizabeth Milne says, "It is true that we share in the lot of fallen man with his tendency to sin, disease and evil, but if we are Christians we also share in the victory of the Passion and Resurrection which has overcome these things and even death itself, once and for all. . . ."[5]

HE BORE OUR SICKNESSES

Matthew relates that one evening Jesus cast out some spirits with a word and that he healed "all who were sick, in order that it

3. TDNT, VII, p. 990.
4. Walter W. Dwyer, *The Churches' Handbook for Spiritual Healing* (New York, 1964), pp. 9, 10.
5. *Ibid.*, p. 11.

might be fulfilled which was spoken through Isaiah the prophet saying, 'He himself took our sicknesses and bore our diseases'" (Matt. 8:16-17). Matthew's quotation is from Isaiah 53:4, part of a chapter which is one of the classic passages for our understanding of the atonement, emphasizing as it does that Christ bore our sins. Matthew is telling us that in bearing our sins Jesus did something about our perennial problem of sickness. Some believers understand the passage to mean that Christ has dealt with our sicknesses in such a way that if we really trust him we will be delivered from all illness; some even go on to rebuke the sick, assuring them that if they had faith they would be cured of every ailment.[6] I cannot find this in Scripture. Paul had his "stake in the flesh" (2 Cor. 12:7), an expression that he does not explain and which has puzzled commentators. But whatever it was, it was certainly a physical ailment of some sort (it was "in the flesh"). Paul wanted to be rid of it and asked the Lord three times that it be taken from him. It may be significant that he asked only three times and then accepted God's answer for him: "My grace is sufficient for you". No matter how great our faith, every ailment is not going to be removed from us in the here and now. Again, Timothy had "frequent infirmities" for which Paul bade him use medical help (1 Tim. 5:23). And we should not forget that Jesus apparently regarded the use of medical help as normal (Matt. 9:12). The New Testament writers never take the line that anyone who really trusts God will never have to endure sickness and pain.

But Matthew is certainly saying that the final answer to our problem with sickness and pain is to be found in the cross. He "was well aware of the Servant's role in Isaiah 53 as one of redemptive suffering . . . and this was the dominant use of the passage in Christian circles. But this did not prevent him noticing that the literal ap-

6. "Any medical attempt at helping would imply a lack of faith in God's healing power. John Alexander Dowie's 1895 sermon entitled 'Doctors, Drugs and Devils; or the Foes of Christ the Healer' illustrates this view that medical means are Satan's instruments to defeat the believer's exercise of true faith" (P. G. Chappell in Walter A. Elwell, ed., *Evangelical Dictionary of Theology* [Grand Rapids, 1984], p. 498).

plicability of Isaiah 53:4 to the healing ministry of Jesus added another dimension to his fulfilment of the mission of God's Servant".[7] We may well reflect that in the final salvation there will be "no more pain" (Rev. 21:4) and that health-giving leaves grow by the "river of the water of life" (Rev. 22:1-2). This surely links up with Paul's words about "the redemption of the body" (Rom. 8:23)—not simply of the soul or spirit, but of the body. The bodily troubles that are so much a feature of this life are not permanent. Christ has won the victory over them all.

Robert Gundry denies that Matthew's meaning is that Jesus "vicariously became sick", and argues that the verbs indicate this. He points out that Matthew replaces the Septuagint's *pherei,* "carries", with *elaben,* "took", for the former "might be taken to imply that Jesus became sick" and he thinks that *ebastasen* "also indicates removal rather than carrying".[8] Richard Gutzwiller makes the important point that sickness was no part of the original creation: "Man came from God's creative hand, healthy in soul and body." He goes on, "It was sin, the mortal sickness of the soul, which first brought sickness of the body as its consequence."[9] This should not be taken to mean that each individual sickness is due to sin. That is contradicted by our experience and is not taught in Scripture; indeed, on occasion it is clearly denied (e.g., John 9:1-3). But we must not go to the other extreme and deny that sin ever leads to

7. R. T. France, *The Gospel according to Matthew* (Leicester and Grand Rapids, 1985), p. 158. France also says, "The Greek words for *took* and *bore* might refer either to undergoing them himself (the primary meaning of the Hebrew) or to removing them (presumably Matthew's thought: he does not suggest that Jesus became sick), but as in Is. 53 the overall concept is of the removal of the people's trouble by the Servant's suffering, the ambiguity is justified" (*ibid.,* p. 159n.).

8. Robert H. Gundry, *Matthew* (Grand Rapids, 1982), p. 150. David Hill understands the verbs to mean "virtually . . . 'to take away, to remove [from the sick]', and therefore 'heal'". He also says, "it seems unlikely that the idea of substitution and the vicarious action of the Servant is entirely absent here" (*The Gospel of Matthew* [London, 1972], p. 161).

9. Richard Gutzwiller, *Day by Day with Saint Matthew's Gospel* (London, 1964), p. 98.

physical troubles. After he had healed the man who had been lame for thirty-eight years Jesus said to him, "Sin no longer, lest something worse happen to you" (John 5:14). Jesus may well be drawing attention to the eternal consequences of sinning and warning the man to live a new spiritual life now that he had a new physical beginning. The possibility cannot be dismissed, however, that he means that a new life of sin would lead to new physical disabilities. On occasion Satan is linked to physical ailments (e.g., Luke 13:16), and we should bear in mind the physical and mental effects of the activities of demons which the Synoptic Gospels so often mention (e.g., Matt. 12:22-28).

There are mysteries here, but what is plain is that sickness does not appear in the original creation story, nor will it remain in the final state of blessedness. Michael Wilson argues that there is an analogy here between sin and sickness. Sin may be "a general term to describe the present condition of the world, and of ourselves in particular; it is the predicament of human beings estranged from God, from the creation and from one another. Creation is spoilt: man is bent." But we may also use the term "to denote a fault for which we are morally responsible". Sickness is similarly a "falling short of the glory of God", and in this aspect we are not responsible for it. We simply share in the plight of all creation. Of course it is possible for us to abuse our bodies, and if we do we bear a moral responsibility for the illness that follows;[10] but we may be ill through no fault of our own. Wilson further points out that "forgiveness of sin is an important part of the healing ministry, not because the sick man is sick through his own fault, but as a step in reconciliation to God and neighbour and self."[11] Those who engage in the ministry of spiritual healing emphasize the importance of repentance and sometimes speak of instances when they preached that people should repent and then found that some had both repented and been healed.

One of the names of God in the Old Testament is "the LORD,

---

10. Michael Wilson, *The Church is Healing* (London, 1966), p. 42.
11. *Ibid.*, p. 44.

your Healer" (Exod. 15:26), and we must remember that he not only "forgives all my sins" but also "heals all my diseases" (Ps. 103:3). The overcoming of sickness may be for the glory of God (John 11:4), for Scripture sees God as in opposition to all such things as disease and sickness. In some way, Scripture seems to be saying, sickness came in at the Fall. It is to be understood not as part of God's good original creation, but as another part of the legacy of human sin.[12] The violation of the laws of health will inevitably result in physical trouble of some sort, so that we may perhaps discern a certain kinship between sickness and sin. At any rate complete healing, making a person "every whit whole", involves dealing with both moral and physical disorder. Looked at in this way it is not at all surprising that Christ's atoning work should have as one of its effects a dealing with sickness, even if we do not see the full effects of that here and now.

THE DEFEAT OF DEATH

Of particular importance is the fact that Christ's saving work includes the defeat of death. Few things are more characteristic of the early Christians than their attitude to death; in fact, it forms a marked contrast to the attitudes prevalent in the pagan world. The tombs of wealthy pagans may be elaborate and richly ornamented, but the inscriptions they bear are universally gloomy. Why not? Death for those pagans was the last enemy, an enemy that no one could overcome. Sooner or later we all succumb. But the Christians believed that Christ's atonement has altered all that. We will die in the sense that we will pass from this present life and our bodies will perish. But Christ's resurrection means that we will

12. Cf. Oscar Cullmann, "the healing miracles are on a par with the forgiveness of sins, since death, to which the *sarx* is fettered, is the result of Adam's sin ('the body is dead because of sin', Rom. 8.10). Thus every disease, while not indeed an individual punishment for some particular sin (John 9.2f.), is, like death, a symptom of the state of general sin in which all humanity is involved" (*The Early Church* [London, 1956], p. 167).

also rise. Death is defeated. The atonement means victory over death.

It is noteworthy that all four Gospels reach their climax with their accounts of the crucifixion and the resurrection. It is true that the teaching of Jesus mattered a good deal to those who recorded it, and it is fair to say that the Person of Christ, the fact that he was both God and man, was of very great importance to them. But what mattered most of all was that Jesus was our Saviour, a fact enshrined in the meaning of his name (Matt. 1:21) and underlined by the final scenes in each of the Gospels. Jesus died to put away our sins and he rose triumphant over death.[13] In our enthusiasm for the resurrection we must not forget that the New Testament attributes saving significance to the death of Jesus. The chapter that above all chapters emphasizes the resurrection also includes the words "Christ died for our sins according to the Scriptures" (1 Cor. 15:3). References to "the blood" of Jesus and picture words like redemption point to the saving death. "The crucifixion is not remembered simply because Jesus had to face Calvary en route to his resurrection. . . . The risen Christ became and remains Redeemer only through his death. The resurrection proved the saving event for the world because of its connection with the death on Calvary."[14]

This is not to minimize the significance of the resurrection. It is indelibly bound up with the saving death, and the two together make up one great act of salvation.[15] This act points to a thorough-

13. Peter Steele brings out the connection between the crucifixion and the resurrection in this way: "It is only if the crucifixion—Christ crucified— is seen as unspeakably outrageous—a situation more squalid and grotesque than one can get straight in words—that there can be any truly good news here at all. If the crucifixion does not become more stunning the more one contemplates it, the resurrection is going to be just a gaudy tail-piece to a hard-luck story" (cited by Gerald O'Collins, *The Easter Jesus* [London, 1973], p. 119).

14. Gerald O'Collins, *The Easter Jesus*, p. 121.

15. Cf. Walther Künneth, "The possibility of a theological inquiry into the saving character of the cross does not exist at all apart from the resurrec-

going defeat of death, for the resurrection was not simply a return to this life, a return that would in due course issue in death. That is what happened to Lazarus and the son of the widow of Nain, as well as to the daughter of Jairus. These people were restored to the life from which they had come, but Jesus rose to a different life. He appeared to his followers from time to time, but he never went back to the life he had lived before. He could conform to this bodily life, as when he invited his followers to feel him and when he ate before them (Luke 24:39-43). But he could also appear among them when the doors were locked (John 20:19), and he could vanish out of their sight (Luke 24:31). He had entered a different mode of being. He had vanquished death and risen to a new and different kind of life. Death had no hold on him (Acts 2:24); he was "the Prince (*archēgos*) of life" (Acts 3:15). He rose to a life that is eternal; death has no place in it.

The triumphant resurrection of Jesus underlies much that is said in the New Testament; it is given classic expression in 1 Corinthians 15. Paul begins a massive argument by pointing to the gospel with its message of Christ's death "for our sins according to the Scriptures" (v. 3), then goes on to his resurrection and his appearances to a number of people. He rejects with decision the views of those who say that "there is no resurrection from the dead" (v. 12), for if that were so Christ would not have risen and that would reduce the whole Christian message to futility (v. 17). He proceeds to contrast Adam and Christ (v. 22); he looks at the final triumph (vv. 24-28), then goes on to contemporary Christian practices that implied resurrection (vv. 29-33) and discusses the nature of the resurrection body (vv. 35-49). He speaks of what will happen at the general resurrection (vv. 50-54), exclaims "Death is swallowed up in victory" (v. 54),[16] and indulges in a little taunt

tion, but is given only in the light of the living Christ. *Thus cross and resurrection stand in the relation of riddle and interpretation*" (*The Theology of the Resurrection* [London, 1965], p. 151).

16. Berkouwer comments, "this is still the most challenging word ever spoken by a human being" (G. C. Berkouwer, *The Work of Christ* [Grand Rapids, 1965], p. 168).

song against death: "Where, death, is your victory? Where, death, is your sting?" He goes on to cry, "Thanks be to God, who gives us the victory through our Lord Jesus Christ" (v. 57).

Throughout this whole discussion Paul is making it clear that, though death seems so powerful to the human race in general and to his contemporaries in particular, it is an important part of understanding the Christian way to see it as totally defeated by Christ.[17] This mortal physical body will indeed perish in the normal way of things, but Paul insists that it will be raised (vv. 42-44). This does not mean that the life of the world to come is a repeat of this life, for Paul insists that there will be change. Even for those who are alive at the time Christ comes back to inaugurate the final state of things there will be change (vv. 51-54). But the important thing is that death is beaten. There is a creative power in Christ's resurrection which means that, while believers will pass through death, this will be no more than the end of this mortal life and the gateway to a new and more wonderful life. This truth is also in mind when Paul writes to the Romans, "he who raised Christ from the dead will give life to your mortal bodies also . . ." (Rom. 8:11). Believers do not have life within themselves in the way Christ has; he could not be held by death (Acts 2:24). But believers will not only be raised; they will be given life, which surely means that they will no longer be subject to death. The victory that Christ won over death has permanent consequences for those who are in Christ.

We should be clear that Paul is teaching that those who are raised will enter life of a different order from this present life. This was not clear to some in the ancient world who looked for resurrection: Paul is not repeating a commonplace. Thus in response to Baruch's question about the shape in which the dead will rise there came the answer: "the earth will surely give back the dead at that

17. "The real *victory* over law, sin, and guilt is given by God *through our Lord, Jesus Christ*. Having received his forgiveness, one no longer need fear death—or anything else. The greatest miracle of all is that a guilty sinner is innocent, and this innocence is a gift given by divine forgiveness worked out by the death and resurrection of Jesus Christ" (William F. Orr and James Arthur Walther, *I Corinthians* [New York, 1976], p. 353).

time; it receives them now in order to keep them, not changing anything in their form. But as it has received them so it will give them back. And as I have delivered them to it so it will raise them" (2 Baruch 50:2; the oracle goes on to show that this will enable people to recognize one another). In the Talmud Queen Cleopatra (not the great queen we associate with Mark Antony) is said to have asked R. Meir, "when they arise, shall they arise nude or in their garments?" His reply likens resurrection to the sprouting of wheat: "if a grain of wheat, which is buried naked, sprouteth forth in many robes, how much more so the righteous, who are buried in their raiment!" (*Sanhedrin* 90b; for this reason some of the Rabbis are said to have been very careful about the robes in which they were to be buried). It is not this kind of resurrection that Paul envisages, but one in which the physical body is transformed into a spiritual body, a suitable vehicle for that life of which he could say, "flesh and blood cannot inherit God's kingdom" (1 Cor. 15:44, 50). The apostle is not referring to a persistence of this life after death but to a victory over death.

A. W. Argyle points out that there are sixty-four references to the resurrection in the New Testament, of which only eight speak of Jesus as rising. The remainder all either say that the Father raised him or they have the passive, "he was raised", which means the same thing.[18] We are to regard the victory, then, as God's victory and as a victory over death, for "Death has been swallowed up in victory" (1 Cor. 15:54). We are to bear in mind that death is "the wages of sin" (Rom. 6:23); thus the victory is not only over physical death but all that "death" can mean. As Ralph Martin puts it, "It is the penalty of sin, not only in that we share mortality with the animals as a biological necessity, but we are 'doomed to die' on account of our sin (Rom. 6:23). Death has become the 'sacrament of sin'; it is the outward and visible sign of a spiritual dis-grace."[19] Death in all its fulness is what Christ has overcome, physical death

18. ET, LXI (1949-50), pp. 187-88.

19. Ralph P. Martin, *The Spirit and the Congregation* (Grand Rapids, 1984), p. 141.

and the death that is the wages of sin. And he has not only "abolished death" but has also "brought life and immortality to light through the gospel" (2 Tim. 1:10). The victory may be associated with the cross rather than the resurrection (e.g., Col. 2:14-15), but we should see it as the same victory: the New Testament writers do not envisage one victory as won by the cross and another by the resurrection. The two are part of one great, divine saving act. Walther Künneth puts it this way, "The death of Jesus procures redemption and reconciliation, it is punishment, sacrifice, a vicarious act, the Crucified is the 'Lamb of God'—all this because in the resurrection God testifies that the fact of the cross is his work, through which he brings the salvation of the world."[20] It is the one God who is at work in the crucifixion and the resurrection, in the lowliness and the glory, in the godforsakenness and the power.

We should not hasten too quickly over Paul's statement that "death has been swallowed up in victory" (1 Cor. 15:54). He is saying something more than that death has ceased for the Christian: he is saying that it has been negated, totally overthrown, its effects wiped out. Christ's victory is complete. Lenski brings out something of the meaning in this way: "Death is not merely destroyed so that it cannot do further harm while all of the harm which it has wrought on God's children remains. The tornado is not merely checked so that no additional homes are wrecked while those that were wrecked still lie in ruin . . . these bodies will be restored, not merely again to be 'flesh and blood,' but henceforth to be incorruptible, immortal, 'spiritual' (v. 44), 'heavenly' (v. 49)."[21] The result of Christ's work is that death has gone, yes. But so has the total effect of death: believers are brought into that glorious life that is not touched by any aspect of death.

The early preaching of the first Christians featured the resur-

20. Walther Künneth, *The Theology of the Resurrection* (London, 1965), p. 155.

21. R. C. H. Lenski, *The Interpretation of St. Paul's First and Second Epistles to the Corinthians* (Minneapolis, 1963), pp. 744f.

rection. Indeed, they could be said to preach "in Jesus the resurrection of the dead" or even "Jesus and the resurrection" (Acts 4:2; 17:18). Indeed, the apostles could say that their function was to bear witness of the resurrection (Acts 1:22; 4:33). Jesus could say that he himself was the resurrection (John 11:25), and a number of times he prophesied that he would rise from the dead (e.g., Mark 8:31; 9:31; Luke 18:33). The resurrection was thus very much in Jesus' mind, something linked firmly with the death he foresaw he would die in due course. All this means that we are to see the victory won over death as a very important feature in the life of the first Christians. We are not to think of it as a peripheral matter, a piece of teaching we may accept or decline as we will. It is at the heart of the faith.[22]

It connects with the life believers live. Paul can speak of his aim to "know him [i.e., Christ] and the power of his resurrection" (Phil. 3:10). The apostle immediately adds, "and the fellowship of his sufferings, being conformed to his death"; the cross is not out of sight when the triumph is in mind. Indeed, James Moffatt could say, "The resurrection of Christ was part of 'the story of the cross'; it belonged to 'the gospel.'"[23] We see this also when Peter speaks of God as "having begotten us to a living hope through the resurrection of Jesus Christ from the dead" (1 Pet. 1:3; cf. 3:21), for he links the Christian's new birth, an essential part of the gospel, to the resurrection. So both the entrance to the Christian life and the continuance of Christian living are linked with Christ's triumph in his death and resurrection (as also in Rom. 6:9-11; Eph. 1:19-20).

22. Gerald O'Collins can say, "In a profound sense Christianity without the resurrection is not simply Christianity without its final chapter. It is not Christianity at all" (*The Easter Jesus*, p. 134).

23. James Moffatt, *The First Epistle of Paul to the Corinthians* (London, 1943), p. 234. T. C. Edwards sees the resurrection as central to our understanding of the gospel: "The resurrection of Christ is the explanation of the entire Gospel. It is the key that unlocks the doctrines, which without it are incredible and unmeaning" (*A Commentary on the First Epistle to the Corinthians* [London, 1885], p. 389).

CHAPTER SEVEN

The Answer to Selfishness

It is natural for every one of us to consider everything we encounter in the light of how it will affect us. I do not mean that we never give thought to other considerations. We all do at times. But what effect a given course of action will have on our own aims and prospects is always a factor of considerable importance. If, as far as we can see, there will be no effect on us, then we find no great difficulty in being objective about it. We then can weigh it up thoughtfully and give a reasoned verdict on its worthwhileness. But where our own interests are involved, we tend to decide questions in the light of what will suit us best. Of course, we do not put it quite like that. We are very good at thinking up respectable reasons for giving our vote to the course that most advances our own self-interest. We discover that it is beneficial to the community, that it is right and just, and, if we are Christians, that it is in line with scriptural teaching. I do not want to be cynical in all this, for I am aware that there are many people for whom altruism is more than a high-sounding word and that it is possible to find people advocating causes that will in fact prove inconvenient to them and disturb their comfort. I am simply drawing attention to a fact of life, that whether we give way to it or not there is always a temptation to let our judgment be coloured by our own self-interest. This is, of course, as old as the human race: there is nothing particularly modern about it.

What is new is the emphasis we give to this factor and the

forms it takes. It is aided in modern times by the fact that more people nowadays give little or no attention to the existence and the demands of God. If anyone holds that there is no God, then, of course, he is not going to give any weight as to whether or not what is proposed is in line with the will of God. Nor will he consider what it means that he is part of the creation of a good God and that one day he will give account of himself to God. He will not see what is proposed as part of the way he serves God or fails in his duty to God.

He may do much the same if he holds that there is a God but is not deeply committed to the service of God. Then, like his atheistic confrere, he will be apt to leave God out of the decision-making process. He will decide on purely human grounds. If he genuinely believes that he is responsible to God, that one day he will give account of himself to his Maker, then he will tend to give more regard to considerations other than those that affect him. I do not, of course, mean that all those who believe in the existence of God do better in their decision-making than others. But it is undeniable that a conviction that one is responsible to God is a brake on some kinds of conduct, and it is a brake that the atheist and the agnostic do not have.

It is, of course, possible that our hypothetical decider will be an altruistically high-minded person, anxious to do what is for the good of other people. But the chances are, in a world like ours, that he won't. The chances are that he will have a deep concern for himself and for his own success and that in the end he will take such action as he thinks will advance his own prosperity. This is a big problem in the modern world, for when a great number of people wholeheartedly and unashamedly follow their own interests there are apt to be clashes. My interests are not necessarily the interests of my neighbour, and if we both resolutely follow what we see as the best course for ourselves, then clashes can easily occur and the results will be unpleasant. I am not arguing that our generation is worse than all others, for I think that human nature has been much the same through the ages. But in modern times, with so many people giving little or no place to the will of God for them, there is a widespread tendency for people to act basically out of a concern for their own interests, quite apart from the interests of others.

One result of this is the cult of violence that is so widespread. There have always been violent men, but I doubt whether in any previous age violence has been so widespread or exercised for so little reason. It happens on a small scale when individual hoodlums decide to do what they want with whoever is unfortunate enough to be within their reach. They may demand money, or perhaps their action is the result of their losing their temper, defending their own piece of turf, expressing their support for their own football team, or any of a multitude of other causes. What they want is all-important. What other people want does not matter. They use their physical strength to tread down opposition and secure their aim. A very distressing feature of modern life is the prevalence of domestic violence. The home has traditionally been a place where all the members are loved and safe and supported. This has probably been exaggerated, and not sufficient notice has been taken of unhappy homes; it is also true that domestic violence has been the easiest to keep hidden, and there may well have been more of it than has been known. But whatever the case in the past, there can be no doubt of its existence in the present. There are all too many homes in which the strongest member, usually the father, inflicts suffering on the others in order to get his own way.

It happens on a large scale when, for example, crime bosses build their empires. The Mafia is contemptuous of the laws of the land and proceeds not on the basis of the common good but on the basis of what the godfathers decide is best for the "family". This opens up the way for all manner of injustice and ill-treatment of those who do not belong. Outside the Mafia as well as inside it there are syndicates specializing in the drug trade, people who are completely indifferent to the misery their practices bring about and completely absorbed in the profits they are able to generate through their operations and the power they can wield.

It happens in the affairs of nations. A nation may be rent by strife; Lebanon in recent years is one example. Or it may be the recipient of troops from an external power, a power that maintains that it is simply assisting the government of the nation, a government that it has instituted and which supports it. And the troops may be stationed there with no attempt to find out what the will of the people is. It is probable that arms sales have never been made on the scale evident in recent years, and those sales point to an uncomfortably large number of weapons being used.

A more sophisticated form of violence may be seen in many of the practices of commerce, as, for example, when the commerce of small nations is harmed and industries perhaps even wiped out in order that the profits of large companies in large nations may be increased. A different form again may be seen in many of the organizations in which ordinary people have their memberships when those who lust after power are able to secure the top positions without regard to the genuine wishes of the majority or the good of the organization as a whole. It is not difficult to find examples of a bad use of the individual's desire for personal aggrandisement. Perhaps we should add here a reference to the protest movements that are so common a feature of modern life in most countries. There is something valuable about such protests because they have a habit of bringing to light wrongs and injustices that would otherwise be covered up, and for that we must all be grateful. But often they go beyond that. Often those who protest, while recognizing that they are in a minority, are bent on forcing the majority to do what they want, and they keep on making things uncomfortable for others until they get their way. There is always a danger when a minority believes firmly that it knows what is best for other people and that it will do them "good" whether they like it or not. Self-aggrandisement can take many forms.

So, too, it is important for Christians to be on their guard against building their own little empires. It is, alas, quite easy for those engaged in Christian work to be more interested in getting their own way than in doing the work of God efficiently and humbly. In church work above all human activities there ought to be cooperation and a readiness to take the lowest place, for by definition those who engage in this kind of service are people who have been saved at great cost by one who for their sakes himself took the lowest place. By definition therefore they are committed to the service of God and bound by what Scripture teaches about the way to serve God. Whatever excuses those outside may give to justify their grabs for power these do not apply to Christians. They of all people should bear in mind that they are accountable to God and that they are doing the work of God, not pursuing personal ambitions.

A CROSS FOR THE CHRISTIAN

We should bear in mind more often than we usually do that Jesus said, "If anyone wills to come after me, let him say 'No' to self and let him take up his cross, daily, and follow me. For whoever wills to save his life will lose it; but whoever loses his life for my sake, this man will save it" (Luke 9:23-24). This is the first mention of the cross in Luke's Gospel, and it must have come as something of a shock to the disciples to have this shameful instrument of execution suddenly introduced as the pattern of service of Christ. The saying is not, of course, to be understood in such a way as to deny the centrality of Jesus' death for our salvation. The Lord is not here affirming that we may merit our salvation by our self-denying service. He is saying that the salvation he brings has implications for the saved. Those who have been saved by the cross of Christ find that they have a cross of their own. The Christian has been crucified with Christ (Gal. 2:19)[1] and buried with him (Rom. 6:4). Salvation by the cross of Christ means relying wholeheartedly on what Christ has done. It means a total rejection of the notion that we can save ourselves by our own merit. It means being humble in the light of the facts (a) that we cannot save ourselves,

1. "As Christ's death was death by crucifixion, the believer is said not only to have died with him but to have been 'crucified with him'. . . . The figure is deliberately bold, designed to emphasize the finality of the death which has put an end to the old order and interposed a barrier between it and the new life in Christ" (F. F. Bruce, *The Epistle to the Galatians* [Grand Rapids and Exeter, 1982], p. 144). Bruce goes on to point out that the perfect tense "emphasizes that participation in the crucified Christ has become the believer's settled way of life".

and (b) that Christ has saved us at great cost to himself. If our will is firmly set on "saving" our life,[2] on making the fullest and richest life we can for ourselves, then by definition we have not entered into the life that Christ has won for us, for that is a life in which we are not set on achieving selfish aims. "A man must spend his life, not hoard it. . . . The Christian must realize that he is given life, not to keep it for himself, but to spend it for others; not to husband its flame, but to burn himself out for Christ and for men."[3]

Let us be clear that Christ is demanding a wholehearted abandonment of selfishness. When he says that his followers must take up their cross, he is using a metaphor for something very difficult and which we often prefer to reduce to something much more manageable. "We all have our cross to bear", we say, when we are referring to the minor troubles that crop up in a normal life, or perhaps we use "our cross" to refer to some particularly burdensome affliction that we must endure. But the people to whom Jesus spoke these words originally would have seen more than that in them. They had actually *seen* men take up their cross. And when a man from their village took up a cross and went off down the track with a little knot of Roman soldiers, they knew he was on a one-way journey. He would not be back. So they knew that Jesus was saying more than "My followers must endure patiently the ordinary hardships of daily life."[4] He was calling for a total abandonment of selfishness. He was speaking of the utmost in self-denial.

2. Cf. R. C. H. Lenski, "By sparing himself this painful denial, this awful cross, he may enjoy every earthly delight and think himself safe, he has thereby really destroyed his very psyche, in which his person dwells: he shall lose it, it is doomed" (*The Interpretation of St. Luke's Gospel* [Minneapolis, 1961], p. 520).

3. William Barclay, *The Gospel of Luke* (Edinburgh, 1967), p. 122. Barclay also says, "The questions are not, 'How much can I *get?*' but, 'How much can I *give?*' Not, 'What is the *safe* thing to do?' but, 'What is the *right* thing to do?'" (*ibid.*).

4. Charles H. Talbert comments, "Bearing the burdens of life is an unlikely interpretation because the cross was not a burden but an instrument of death . . . there is nothing and no one to whom there can be permanent attachment except the one who goes before carrying his cross" (*Reading Luke* [New York, 1984], p. 107).

The New Testament writers have a number of ways of bringing out the truth that the Christian way is not the way of the world with a few of its bad habits dusted off: it is a radically new way. So they may speak of repentance, the total abandonment of the evil in our lives.[5] Or it is conversion, a turning away from the old and a setting forward resolutely on a new direction (Acts 3:19). There is a new creation (2 Cor. 5:17; Gal. 6:15), for what is being attempted in the Christian life is not something that can be done without divine aid, and divine aid which re-creates the whole person. It is a dying to sin (Rom. 6:2), or a dying with Christ (Rom. 6:8), even a being crucified with him (Gal. 2:19), a being baptized into his death (Rom. 6:3). It means being buried with Christ (Rom. 6:4) and being risen with Christ (Col. 3:1). It means "always carrying in the body the dying of Jesus" so that "the life of Jesus may be manifested in our body" (2 Cor. 4:10). It is a putting off of the old man and a putting on of the new (Eph. 4:22-24), even a crucifying of the old man (Rom. 6:6). It is a daily dying (1 Cor. 15:31). It is a being born all over again (John 3:3, 5, 7). We should be in no doubt but that being saved by the cross of Christ has the most far-reaching effects on the whole of the life of the saved. That there is a cross for the Christ means that there is a cross for the Christian.

PUNISHMENT

Being forgiven does not mean a license to return to the sins of which one has been forgiven, but an abandonment of them. It involves seeing sin as the serious thing it is. This involves us in an ef-

---

5. The use the Christians made of the concept of repentance was distinctive. J. Behm points out that in ordinary Greek usage the word points to a change of mind but the change may be "for the bad as well as the good". And it always refers to "an individual instance of change of judgment or remorse in respect of a specific act which is now no longer approved. . . . For the Greeks *metanoia* never suggests an alteration in the total moral attitude, a profound change in life's direction, a conversion which affects the whole of conduct" (TDNT, IV, p. 979). In the New Testament the term points to a change which radically alters the whole life.

fort, for in a modern community sin is for the most part not taken seriously. It is reduced to an unfortunate mishap, perhaps the result of a deplorable heredity or of a disastrous environment, or of a sad coming together of provocative events. This means that the sinner is more sinned against than sinning, and it means that punishment is rarely seen as merited, but rather as reformatory or perhaps as a deterrent. Indeed, to regard it as merited is often held to be something taken out of the dark ages, a relic of primitive thinking that we should have abandoned long ago. It is seen as vindictive, as the assertion of a primitive lust for vengeance. The case is rarely argued; it is simply stated with the utmost dogmatism. But there are good reasons for seeing this as a facile assumption and one with unfortunate consequences. The fact is that unless the offender can say, "I *deserved* that punishment", it is unlikely that he will be reformed and perhaps improbable that he will be deterred.

I have never seen any real attempt to deal with the position taken up by writers like F. R. Bradley and C. S. Lewis that punishment is essentially retributive.[6] Penologists usually dismiss this as outdated and put their emphasis on the reform of the criminal. Nobody surely would want to overlook the importance of reform, but to insist that this is the central thing is to overlook some important considerations. One is that it puts a good deal of trust in the

6. Hodgson cites Bradley for a significant part of his argument (*The Doctrine of the Atonement*, pp. 54f.). Lewis wrote an article entitled "The Humanitarian Theory of Punishment" which was published in *Twentieth Century*, III, no. 3, and reprinted in *Res Judicatae*, 6, no. 2, and in *The Churchman*, LXXIII, pp. 55ff. Interestingly he concludes with "One last word. You may ask why I send this to an Australian periodical. The reason is simple and perhaps worth recording. I can get no hearing for it in England." His view, it would seem, is not to be heard in some circles. In another Australian periodical John Kleinig has an article entitled "Punishment in Philosophical and Biblical Perspective" (*Interchange*, 3, no. 1 [1971], pp. 29-45). He argues "that punishment is taken to be justified because it is the just suffering of the wrongdoer. Another way of saying this is to maintain that the wrongdoer deserves punishment" (p. 33). That is important for an understanding of the biblical position.

reliability of the would-be reformer. Why should the criminal come to conform to the standards of the reformer? What is there about one man that gives him the right to demand that another should conform to his standards? We can, of course, remove the burden from the shoulders of the individual reformer and speak of the standards of the community, but the offender may still ask why he should conform to other people's standards. Communities have been known to be wrong.

Problems arise also if the attempt is made to act consistently according to this principle. Thus a man may commit some minor crime, say petty theft, and prove very resistant to attempts to reform him. His persistence means that his punishment must be carried on indefinitely, whereas the man may well feel, and those who observe the scene may agree with him, that he has been punished enough for a comparatively small offence. At the other end of the scale someone may commit a major crime, say murder, and may reform immediately. If it becomes obvious that the public is in no danger, for this man will never kill again, is he to be released forthwith with no punishment whatever?

It is not much better with deterrence. If a certain punishment deters others from committing a particular crime, well and good. But if it does not deter people, then why continue with it? And the fact is that the continuing existence of criminals shows that a good deal of punishment does not in fact deter.[7]

Those who advocate punishment for reformatory and deterrent considerations only do not seem to give attention to the fact that when someone being punished feels that what is being done to him is unjust the punishment neither reforms nor deters him: it in-

7. J. Arthur Hoyles notices a variety of views of punishment and shows that deterrence does not work: "It has been used to justify the most savage penalties without achieving the desired end" (*Punishment in the Bible* [London, 1986], p. 119). It is no better with reform, for "Penologists are talking of the collapse of the rehabilitation ideal" (p. 122). His own view is that "The ultimate penal reform must be the abolition of punishment", and he goes on to envisage "the day when therapy will replace the system of punishment" (p. 139).

furiates him. If a punishment is to reform or to deter, the offender must be brought to realize that his sin, his own sin, is coming home to him; he is getting what he deserves.

FORGIVENESS

The Christian doctrine of forgiveness takes sin seriously. God does not forgive with a wave of the hand as though to say, "It does not matter much". To bring about forgiveness God, in the person of his Son, came to this earth and took on himself the penalty of our sin. From one point of view the cross means the recognition that sin is serious, that it *deserves* punishment, and that the Son of God stood in our stead so that we will never undergo that punishment. He absorbed our sin with its consequences, took on him all that it involves.

This is in contrast with the way it so often happens in our affairs. Let me illustrate. Suppose that I do you a wrong, perhaps that I call you a nasty name and give you a nasty punch. That would be a very bad thing. You would feel aggrieved and you might well retaliate by doing the same to me, and that would be worse (certainly I would think so!). You would be doubling the amount of evil in the situation and provoking me to go further. There might be no end to the evil.

But perhaps you would not retaliate. Perhaps you would say, "This poor Australian. He probably does not know better. That, I suppose, is the kind of thing they are always doing down there. I'm not going to get caught up in a fight or a slanging match. I forgive him freely." In that case do you see what you have done? You have taken my evil action, which could have provoked a chain of evil events, and absorbed it. At cost to yourself you have eliminated the possibility of a chain of evil happenings. You have suffered in your person the evil I have done. In doing so you have turned something evil into the raw material for something fine and good—forgiveness. It can be the same with all manner of evil deeds.

Leonard Hodgson uses the illustration of a man ruined by his partner's absconding with the firm's funds, leaving him "in comparative penury" and "saddled with serious liabilities towards clients". He could say, "I've been a fool. I see now that in this world it doesn't pay to be honest and trusting. I don't see why my wife and family should lose so much by this. I don't see why we should have to pay the cost of this fellow's dishonesty. If I can't get it back from him, I'll get it from others. I've learned my lesson. I won't again make the mistake of trusting anyone, and I can see lots of ways in which I've been too scrupulous in the past. I won't do that again." In that case the evil and misery that he has experienced will go on in ever widening circles. He will have multiplied the evil and ensured that it continues.

But he need not do this. Hodgson considers it possible that he might say: "This is a challenge to all that I stand for in human relationships and business morality. Whatever it may cost us, my family and me, we must not let this make us bitter or resentful, cynical or unscrupulous. This is an opportunity of showing that in professing to voyage through life under the flag of Christ we are not merely 'fair-weather sailors'."[8] To absorb the evil and to live unselfishly will be costly, but it is the way evil will be defeated.

So with the person who lies to us or who robs us and so on. Day by day we are faced with situations in which wrong has been done to us in small matters or great and where our reaction carries the possibility of increasing the amount of evil or of increasing the amount of good. Wherever evil is done to us we are faced with the possibilities of either multiplying the evil or of absorbing it and using it to promote what is good.

Part of Christ's atonement can be understood from this point of view. "When he was abused, he did not abuse in return, when he suffered he did not threaten, but commended himself to him that judges righteously. Who himself bore our sins in his body on the tree . . ." (1 Pet. 2:23). Here is a plain statement of Jesus' refusal to retaliate; he simply took what people did to him in silence. Surely we are to say that in Christ God absorbed the evil that people had

8. Leonard Hodgson, *The Doctrine of the Atonement* (London, 1951), pp. 61, 62.

done. We must not think that God was indifferent when the people he made turned aside from right paths into sin of various kinds. No. "His heart was filled with pain" (Gen. 6:6). And we must not think that his grief is aroused only by sin done directly against him, such as blasphemy. An important insight is revealed in David's prayer, "Against you, you only, have I sinned and done what is evil in your sight" (Ps. 51:4). Most of us would think that David sinned against people since adultery and murder were involved. But whatever the sin against people, there is always a greater element of sin against God when we defy him and break the laws he has given for our conduct.

It would have been possible for God simply to have punished evildoers, which, of course, means all of us. But instead he sent his Son. We might have expected the world to welcome the Son of God and to follow his teaching. But it did not. The world rejected him and put him on a cross. It did its worst to him. He could have retaliated. He reminded Peter that he could have asked his Father for more than twelve legions of angels (Matt. 26:53), which would have been more than enough to deal with Pilate and the Jews. But he did not retaliate. He bore the sin of the world, absorbed it in his Person.[9] He did not multiply the evil brought into being by the sin of the world, but took it on himself, took it out of the way by suffering it in his own Person. Margaret Dewey speaks of Jesus' authority as "the authority of the Lamb of God, who has perceived that the only way to take away the sin of the world without compounding it is to '*take* it': to accept personal responsibility, to 'carry the can', to be the butt of everyone's resentments, to accept all that others project upon him—to absorb the impact of sin

9. Cf. C. F. D. Moule, ". . . the holy God himself met the sin, accepted its entail, entered into its costliness, suffered redemptively in his own Son. Then at least it became clear—however mysterious and unsearchable God's ways must always remain to us—that here was no overlooking of guilt or trifling with forgiveness; no external treatment of sin, but a radical, a drastic, a passionate and absolutely final acceptance of the terrible situation, and an absorption by the very God himself of the fatal disease so as to neutralise it effectively" (*The Sacrifice of Christ* [London, 1957], p. 28).

without fighting back. Only so can the vicious circle of action and reaction be broken."[10] This is not the whole truth about the atonement, but it is an important part of the truth.

Another way of looking at it may perhaps be suggested by the application to God of the imagery of childbirth. God says, through the prophet, "For a long time I have kept silent, I have been quiet and held myself back. But now, like a woman in childbirth, I cry out, I gasp and pant" (Isa. 42:14). Frances Young links this passage with that in which God says, "you forgot the God who gave you birth" (Deut. 32:18), and thinks there may be an implication "that this labour of God's is a labour to bring forth a new people".[11] Can we say that the cross is God absorbing the evil in the world he had made and bringing to birth, at cost to himself, a new people, a people of God cleansed from their sins? God, so to speak, takes responsibility for the world he has made, a world which exercised its freedom by going from sin to sin, from evil to evil. God could have blotted out all evildoers in mighty judgment, but instead he bore the sins of his people and thus opened the way for a new world, a new people.

We should not take a negative view of divine forgiveness. It is easy to see that sin brings about a difficult and troubled situation and to understand forgiveness as a palliative. It removes the difficulty and the trouble and thus restores the former state of affairs. But should we not rather regard forgiveness as creative? As having the potentiality for something quite new, a re-shaping of the future in a new and better way? David Atkinson can say: "Forgiveness is a dynamic concept of change. It refuses to be trapped into a fatalistic determinism. It acknowledges the reality of evil, wrong and injustice, but it seeks to respond to wrong in a way that is creative of new possibilities. Forgiveness signals an approach to wrong in terms, not of peace at any price, not of a destructive intention to destroy the wrongdoer, but of a willingness to seek to reshape the future in the light of the wrong, in the most creative way pos-

10. *Thinking Mission*, 43 (Summer 1984), p. 3.
11. *Can These Bones Live?* p. 48.

sible."[12] God's absorption of the evil does not bring back the status quo. It makes something completely new. The Bible does not envisage forgiveness as taking us back to the Garden of Eden, but on to the City of God.

This way of looking at the cross brings out some important truths. It insists that God absorbs the worst that sin can do and therefore that nothing can stand against his purpose of love. Since it is God who is absorbing the evil, there is an infinite capacity for this absorption and we need not fear that one day there will be an evil too big to cope with. It is impossible to envisage a greater evil than the evil that took place when created beings who professed to be the servants of God took the Son of God and put him on a cross. Nothing can ever prevail against the love displayed at the cross. And if God reacts towards evil in this way, then a good deal of the task of the servant of God is marked out for him. It is the duty of the church and all its members to live as the forgiven community; each of us is to take up a cross in following Christ (Luke 9:23). That means that we are to live in a spirit of forgiveness and in this way to absorb evil and to forgive. It is our task constantly to take the world's evil and to use it as the raw material for something good. The world may or may not respond to what we are doing. That is not our business. But forgiving others and refusing to multiply evil by reacting to it in a spirit of anger or hatred or a spirit of paying back injuries is. That's what taking up a cross means, and it is in this way that by God's grace we limit the extent and the power of evil.

12. Cited in John R. W. Stott, *The Cross of Christ* (Leicester, 1986), p. 310.

Conclusion

These studies are not in any sense a survey of New Testament teaching on the cross. I have tried to do such a survey in an earlier book, *The Cross in the New Testament* (Grand Rapids, 1965). Nor is it a survey of the theories whereby godly Christians through the ages have tried to interpret the meaning of Christ's sufferings for them in their situation. In Chapter Two I have drawn attention to what seem to be the principal ways in which the atonement has been understood. That examination is not, of course, exhaustive, but it does, I think, show that each of the theories has made a particular appeal to people in a particular age. It has also, I trust, made it clear that no theory so far put forward has been able to explain the atonement wholly. How can any theory possibly do this? The atonement is unique. There is nothing like it. When we speak of Christ's saving death, we are speaking of a mighty act of God without parallel.

Our theories are of value in that they draw attention to important aspects of Christ's saving work. The parable of the blind men telling what an elephant is like is useful. One, obviously standing near a leg, likened the animal to a tree trunk. A second, standing near the body, said it was like a barrel. The third, whose position was near the trunk, maintained that the animal was something like a flexible tube. Each of course was correct, but equally each was incorrect because his explanation dealt only with that part of the elephant with which he was confronted. It is like that with our theories. Each of them draws attention to something that is true, and not only true but valuable. We need the insight that the atonement is a victory over evil, we need the insight that it is the payment of our penalty, and we need the insight that it is the outpouring of love that inspires us to love in return. The atonement is all of these, and we neglect any of them to our impoverishment.

May I make my protest against the way the penal theory is neglected in much modern discussion. It is, of course, possible to state it in such a way that it is simply repulsive. In these days when our distaste for legalism is such that a legalist has lost his case before he opens his mouth it is easy to maintain that it puts too much emphasis on law, not love. When it appears obvious to almost everyone that love is the greatest thing, it is not difficult to argue that anything we cannot equate easily with love is suspect. But none of this gets to the root of the matter.

What is of deep concern to many faithful believers is the way those who argue against the penal view neglect the truth that Christianity is concerned with what is right. Christianity is concerned with many other things too, of which love is a very important one. I trust that I will not be accused of taking lightly the fact that God is love. After all, I have written a whole book on what the Bible says about love and in it I have stressed that nothing is more important than the love of God and nothing is more important in living the Christian life than love to God and love to our fellow-Christians and love to others in our community. But when we have said "God is love", we have not said everything that is important about the atonement. We may well have said what is most important, but we have not said it all.

In a day like ours it can scarcely be denied that the importance of doing what is right needs emphasis. Many, perhaps all, of our many and varied troubles arise from wrongdoing of one sort or another. If Christians lose sight of the truth that God is concerned with the right and for the right, we are settling for a mini-Christianity. And what the New Testament writers are saying (among other things) is that when God sent his Son to die on the cross for our salvation he was concerned with the right. Somehow it was right that he should save in this way. Surely God is powerful enough to save, so to speak, with a wave of the hand, with one saving word. Why then did he bother to send his beloved Son? And why did that Son die the most painful and shameful of deaths? Part of the reason, the New Testament writers are saying, was because right was upheld in saving people in this way. Sinners *deserved* to die, and Christ made himself one with sinners. Would it be easier if we thought of the goodness of God? Surely nobody is going to dispute the proposition that God is good, but would it be a good action to bring about the salvation of evil people in a way that took no cognizance of the wrong they have done? The love and the mercy of God are to be given emphasis, but so is his goodness. If God is not good, what do we have left? And the New Testament insists that God saves in a way that is good and just as well as loving and merciful. We must beware of trying to sell God short in affirming his love and his mercy while denying his goodness and his justice.

Traditionally evangelical Christians have said that right was upheld in that the penalty of breaking the divine law was paid. Perhaps we can discover it also in some of the things I have argued in this book. The right was upheld when God took action to overcome the futility that is written over so much of life. Scripture does not suggest that the futility is in any sense due to God, but perhaps we could say that in dealing with futility God is doing what is right with the creation he has brought about. He made this universe and this human race in such a way that sin could result, and in fact sin did result. In that situation frustration and futility were inevitable. And in saving men from that kind of situation God did what was right.

That, it seems to me, is important. And this little book arises because I also consider it important that we should not see the traditional theories as saying all that needs to be said about the cross. There are depths here that we have not explored. From the New Testament it is clear that the redemption of the body is with a view to the removal of futility among other things. That should speak eloquently to an age in which frustration and futility have emerged as major obstacles in the way of living a full and satisfying life.

So with ignorance. We are all impressed with the advance our generation has made in areas like science and technology. But this does not mean that we are all budding Einsteins. We are only too well aware of our limitations and our all-too-frequent dependence on technicians for the simplest of repairs. We have immense knowledge available to us through the wonderful libraries that figure so largely in advanced countries, and in addition the media bring before us more information than we can assimilate. But in the face of all this what matters to many of us is the football scores! We are content to remain ignorant of many things, and our ignorance in matters religious is abysmal. It is important that Christ's atoning work has brought us the knowledge of God, a knowledge we could never attain left to our own devices. But we are not left to our best guesses. In the cross we have been given a wonderful revelation. We have been given the gift of eternal life, that life which means knowing God.

The sense of living in a godforsaken world oppresses many. Sometimes their problem is caused by the evils we do to one another, sometimes by our helplessness in the face of natural disasters. Many of us are left wondering where God is at such times. It is salutary to reflect that Jesus knew the sense of being godforsaken, and that, indeed, it was in and through that experience that he brought us salvation. Our understanding of the atonement is impoverished unless we see that it included the overcoming of what it is to be forsaken by the Father.

Sickness and death are ever with us. I imagine that most people, at any rate in the advanced countries, think of sickness as being steadily overcome in the hands of our medical researchers. We are aware of the fact that there are many sicknesses for which we have at present no cures, but we feel that the onward march of medical research will surely provide whatever cures we need. Perhaps that should be modified in view of the spread of AIDS, for some prominent medical authorities have said that they despair of our ever being able to find a way to overcome this deadly disease.

And certainly nobody can do anything in the face of death. We know that as long as this earth lasts the human race will be mortal. So we need the assurance that in the cross there is healing. Few things are as distinctive of Christianity as its view of death. In the first century death was feared. It was the end of everything, and nothing could be done about it. But for the Christians it was not the end; it was the beginning. The resurrection of Jesus carried with it the resurrection of believers. Death has been swallowed up in victory.

This is not an altruistic age. There are conspicuous exceptions, and we all admire altruism when we see it in others. But displaying it ourselves is quite another matter. It is so easy to concentrate on self, and most people today seem to do just that. In the cross we see the negation of self-assertion, and we need the reminder that we are to take up our own cross and walk in the way of the Christ. Instead of retaliating when he was ill-treated, Jesus absorbed in himself the worst the world could do to him and made it the raw material for the greatest good the world has seen.

In all this we discover that the atonement is vaster and deeper than any of the traditional theories affirms. I am not suggesting that we jettison any of them. I gladly affirm what they affirm. But I want to go on from there to say that Scripture gives us grounds for affirming that there are other things that the atonement effects, some of which are very important for twentieth-century citizens. It is well if we enlarge our horizons to embrace them.